D1501593

What's
Your
Heaven?

Also by Rebecca Rosen

What the Dead Have Taught Me About Living Well

Awaken the Spirit Within

Spirited

What's Your Heaven?

7 LESSONS TO HEAL THE PAST AND LIVE FULLY NOW

Rebecca Rosen

With Samantha Rose

HARPER WAVE

An Imprint of HarperCollinsPublishers

All identifying information, including names and other details, has been changed to protect the privacy of individuals. Any similarity to actual individuals or families is coincidental.

WHAT'S YOUR HEAVEN?. Copyright © 2023 by Rebecca Rosen. All rights reserved. Printed in the United States of America. No part of this book may be used or reproduced in any manner whatsoever without written permission except in the case of brief quotations embodied in critical articles and reviews. For information, address HarperCollins Publishers, 195 Broadway, New York, NY 10007.

HarperCollins books may be purchased for educational, business, or sales promotional use. For information, please email the Special Markets Department at SPsales@harpercollins.com.

FIRST EDITION

Artwork by TairA/Shutterstock, Inc.

Library of Congress Cataloging-in-Publication Data has been applied for.

ISBN 978-0-06-327254-5

23 24 25 26 27 LBC 5 4 3 2 1

This book is for you, the reader, and for everyone who is as much a part of my soul contract as I am yours. Thank you for being on this journey with me as we continue to courageously work together to cocreate a heavenly life.

Contents

...

AUTHOR'S NOTE xi

INTRODUCTION: WORKING FOR THE WEEKEND 1

Part I Welcome to Earth School

....

CHAPTER 1

Everyone Gets Study Hall

9

CHAPTER 2

Progress Report

29

Part II Check Your Source

....

CHAPTER 3

I AM Connected

57

CHAPTER 4

I AM Remembering

86

CHAPTER 5

I AM Supported; I AM Surrounded

119

Part III Independent Study Hall

• • • •

CHAPTER 6
I AM Worthy
151

CHAPTER 7
I AM Here to Heal + Contribute
174

Part IV Pick a Study Partner

• • • •

CHAPTER 8
I AM Learning from Others + I AM Teaching Others
197

CHAPTER 9
Share Your Notes
244

Graduation Day Rainbow Meditation
253

ACKNOWLEDGMENTS 259
STUDY GUIDE: CONVERSATION QUESTIONS FOR LIFE REVIEW
263

Author's Note

. . .

Before we dive in, I want to take a brief moment to touch on the language you'll find throughout this book. *Spirit* is the word I use to identify something that you may have another term for—such as God, Goddess, Higher Power, Creator, the Universe, the Divine, Supreme Being, Source, or All Love. In my second book, *Awaken the Spirit Within*, I dropped G-O-D into the conversation within the first few pages, only to hear from readers that my easy-breezy use of the word felt a little heavy-handed, even triggering to them, so I've since adjusted. I want to be very clear on this point: it's not my intention to challenge *or* validate your belief system, but only to share the messages and insights that the departed confirm for me daily.

I liken Spirit to an energetic source of heart-pumping love and light, burning and vibrating with powerful and radiant intensity. Because everything—external and internal—is made up of energy that never dies but simply changes form, then it naturally follows that you and me, every one of us, are in our simplest form, walking, talking, and breathing extensions of Spirit.

In the pages ahead, I will use the following terms and often interchangeably. These are terms that I have grown to reference

XII · *Author's Note*

over the years based on information I've been shown from the Spirit world:

Spirit: (with a capital *S)* is the most powerful energy source, radiating at the highest frequency of love. We are all connected to Spirit and interconnected to each other as individual "sparks" of Spirit.

Team Spirit: Our own personal support system that guides us as we journey through life, comprised of angels, guides, and deceased loved ones, along with our "ground crew," which includes your living family and friends from whom you learn and teach valuable life lessons. (Much more on this is to come.)

spirit: (with a lowercase *s*) refers to our eternal, energetic life force in a human body and our nonhuman energetic presence that resides in the Spirit world (aka the nonhuman presence of our deceased loved ones).

spirit guides: Our spirit guides frequently work in tandem with our deceased loved ones to support us through challenging periods of our lives. In general, spirit guides tend to be spirits in between lifetimes who "drop in" with us at different times, depending on the lesson or assignment we are learning.

soul: Our eternal life force or the energetic essence of our spirit that incarnates into a body and that leaves the body upon physical death. Once back in the Spirit world, our soul is often referred to as our "spirit."

I will also reference the many ways that spirits communicate with me, and not just me, but also how they can communicate with *you.* Spirits communicate through our senses, also called our "clairs"—what we're feeling, sensing, hearing, and seeing.

Clairvoyance means "clear seeing," and people who are highly visual—such as artists, builders, photographers, and designers and those who are able to understand an idea best when they *see it* written, projected, sketched, or drawn—tend to better attune to spirit energy this way.

If you best retain and comprehend information when you *hear* it spoken aloud or through music and sound, you may be **clairaudient**. People with a clear sense of hearing are often musicians, singers, writers, and public speakers.

Or perhaps you're more emotionally oriented. Doctors, therapists, teachers, and those who are natural caregivers and healers tend to have a clear sense of feeling called **clairsentience**.

Finally, there are those of us who just *know* things. We feel certainty in our bones. Answers come to us in an instant. We don't deliberate for long; we "go with our gut" or act on a "strong hunch." This clear sense of knowing is called **claircognizance**, and people with this sense are highly intuitive and often have an open channel to spirit energy.

While most of us have a dominant *clair*, they are all equally accessible, we can all develop this sixth sense. Like building muscles, we can build our sensory strength to interpret messages from beyond. It takes practice, and the more you practice asking for guidance and following it (key!), the stronger your connection will become to the Other Side, and the language of Spirit will become second nature.

Signs: Spirits also communicate with the living by manipulating our physical and mental experience in ways that they anticipate will grab your attention and resonate with you. Examples of physical signs are found objects; unexpected electrical occurrences; sparks or flashes of light in photography; birds, insects, and

XIV · *Author's Note*

animals showing up in profound moments; and synchronicities. Examples of mental signs are dream visitations; inspired thoughts and feelings (seemingly out of nowhere!); ears ringing; and waking up with a meaningful song or lyric in your head. I've developed my own "sign language" over the years that includes numbers, patterns, symbols, and both physical and mental phenomenon, and you can also build your own vocabulary of signs that spirits can use to directly communicate with you. While they can be easy to dismiss at first, signs often increase in frequency when they are acknowledged, and continually requested. (More on signs in Chapter 5.)

Reading: Whether it is one-on-one, with a small group, or in a large audience setting, when I give a reading, I am serving as a medium or a *bridge* between this world and the next, where I use a combination of my clair senses to download and interpret meaningful messages from spirits and other enlightened beings and impart them to the living.

Bonus Material: Throughout the pages ahead, you will find this icon to indicate that there is bonus material related to the content you're reading in the form of audible meditations, instructional videos, and assessments. This complimentary material is available to you by using the QR code at the back of the book.

What's
Your
Heaven?

Working for the Weekend

...

If we haven't yet met—in the pages of one of my books, online, or in real life—let me introduce myself: my name is Rebecca Rosen. I'm a spiritual medium who connects the living with those who have departed from this Earth. I've spent the past twenty-two years on a wondrous and magical journey, speaking to individuals, intimate groups, and large audiences from all over the world who are openhearted, curious, and sometimes skeptical about *what comes next*. I've written three books in an attempt to answer some of life's biggest questions and to empower my readers with the skills to connect with their own intuitive knowing and interpret signs from their departed loved ones who are still very much with them, in real time, and who are eager to share their support and guidance.

My life has changed a lot since I wrote my last book, *What the Dead Have Taught Me About Living Well*. My husband, Chris, and

I now have a houseful of five teenagers—two from my previous marriage and three from his—plus a spirited six-year-old between us, who came along unexpectedly. As a woman who likes to keep things relatively chill when I'm out of the office, that's a lot of frenetic energy to get used to (especially on Sunday nights, when one or more of the kids inevitably "remembers" that they have a homework assignment due on Monday).

On such a recent night, my oldest son, Jakob, who's an aspiring filmmaker at the age of seventeen, was finishing up the edits on his movie project due the next day. This project was a big deal—his film would debut to a crowd of over two hundred people at a downtown theater—and he'd been working on it for many months. And yet here he was, still tinkering with the sound quality. He was frantic. "Mom, what if I can't get it done in time?" I felt for him, I mean, *I really did.* My psychic senses picked up on his anxiety and I could clairvoyantly "see" his fear: a packed auditorium of people and nothing to show them. I stood in the doorway of his room, filled with a mother's empathy while simultaneously trying to hold my tongue. *He'd had months to get this done!* I was about to leave him to it when my own parents' advice slipped from my lips before I could stop it: "You know, Jakob, if you hadn't waited until the last minute, then you wouldn't be in this situation. I wish you could have wrapped this up on Friday." No sooner did these words of wisdom hit the air between us than I caught myself. *Wait, did I really just say that?* I was a teenager once and a good student, but I don't remember ever sitting down to complete homework on a Friday night. *As if!* Of course, I kept this rewind moment to myself as Jakob rolled his eyes at me and mumbled, "Super helpful, Mom," before returning to his work.

And this got me thinking: all of us show up in this life with assignments. Mending complicated relationships with parents, reconciling with estranged friends, learning the tough lesson of standing up for our worth at work, identifying how to best fit in within our social groups and contribute to our larger community. Our assignments, or in my business, our "soul contracts," are deliberately set in place to help us learn important truths before we leave this life, or we're destined to get the same homework—the same messy interactions, clumsy missteps, frustrating relationships, and challenging tests—all over again in the next.

That's right, you don't graduate with your soul's hard-earned diploma at the end of your life. Your work continues on the Other Side. Now don't roll your eyes at me like Jakob did. I promise to unpack the implications of an extended school day in the many pages ahead. And anyway, there's a workaround. It's the same advice I offered Jakob: *What if you did your homework on Friday afternoon?* Not later, in the eleventh hour on a Sunday night? Today. Imagine what it would feel like to have the hard work of your life completed and out of the way. No more scores to settle. All manner of debts resolved. Overdue apologies delivered. Wounds, deep and surface, healed. Imagine what that would feel like. Imagine a newfound sense of peace and resolve. The relief of reconciliation. The satisfaction of clarity and closure.

Doesn't that sound like a little slice of heaven?

That's what this book is about—getting ahead of your assignments so that you can enjoy your life today . . . *right here, right now.*

As a spiritual medium, I've made it my life's work to normalize the paranormal, and to pass on messages of reconciliation, hope, and healing from the unseen world. I'm flooded with messages every day from beyond that provide validation to the living that our loved ones are not dead and gone, not really. They're alive and well in another form, one that resides on a different frequency, at a higher vibration, in an alternate "cloud," if you will, and still connected, and accessible, to us forever. These spirits offer comfort, relief, and resolution to their living loved ones by imprinting words, sayings, symbols, initials, numbers and dates, threads of conversations, music lyrics, and images that flash in my mind like a daydream, along with intense *feelings* that flood my body or pop into my mind with a deep *knowing* that I translate to people in real time. As a medium, it's my honor to lift the veil for people hungry for spiritual truth and a deeper understanding of life after death. Day after day, spirits line up outside my mental door, eager and excited to share their insights. And as soon as I invite them in, one of their favorite topics of conversation is to describe where they are now.

Ready for it?

Most of our departed loved ones reveal that they're somewhere that can easily be described as *heavenly* and yet, the big reveal is that heaven isn't a physical place. For those of you who may have always questioned the logistics or coordinates of heaven, this may come as validating news. For others who struggle with the imagery of pearly gates, or who never bought into the concept of a sacred destination described by the Christian church as a place souls go if they're "good," what I'm about to say next may offer some relief. None of us need to cross over, choose a side, climb a staircase—or go anywhere—to experience a heavenly existence. Because heaven is a *state of being* that is ruled by feelings of peace and contentment, connection, bliss, oneness, freedom, relief, and joy. And love. So much love.

If this is true—and the departed I've communicated with in-sist that it is—then we don't have to wait until we're no longer in a physical body to experience the serenity of heaven. We can each find more peace, happiness, and contentment right now, in this life. While I hope this is encouraging news, understand that this alignment between heaven and Earth doesn't just happen. It requires effort. And that's where doing your homework comes in.

Think of it this way—all of us living beings are students in Earth School. We are each assigned a unique lesson plan, on which we are routinely tested and presented with learning opportunities to advance and excel. Assuming we show up for class, do our home-work, and turn in our assignments, then a solid "A for effort" is ours to have. Sounds doable, right?

It is . . . except that many, if not most, of us resist, sidestep, post-pone, or altogether forget to engage in the work that's ours to do. We don't put forth our best effort, and this lapse has consequences.

For starters, when we fail to engage with the lessons essen-tial to our spiritual growth and evolution, we stagnate—we may find ourselves eking out a life in a hard and frustrating place. We may be spinning our wheels, endlessly stuck at the same unmoving pace, repeating messy interactions, struggling in rela-tionships, taking clumsy missteps, trudging along an unfulfilling work path, or not moving forward at all. Second, when we show up late to class, *or never show up at all*, we must repeat the same assignments. In readings, when I tap into my intuitive senses and clairvoyantly "see" a spirit sitting at a school desk and feeling nagging guilt or regret, that's my sign that they didn't complete an important life lesson, and they continue to be tasked with it in the spiritual realm. Spirits come through in readings loud and clear, urging their still-living loved ones to: *Do your work now. Do not put it off until later.*

So, take a minute and think about it: What's your current standing in Earth School? Are you at the top of your class? Barely passing? Coasting in the middle? Planning to cram on Sunday night? Wherever you are now, this book has something for you. Based on my experiences communicating with enlightened beings in the spiritual realm, I will share what I've learned about life assignments. And while I can't do your homework *for you*, I can help you identify where you might be tripped up, stuck, or stalled. And once the hard work is out of the way, you can spend more of your time Earthside enjoying the feeling of heaven.

Part I

Welcome to
Earth School

CHAPTER 1

Everyone Gets Study Hall

• • •

Life is always filled with challenges, but as I write this book,
the past couple of years—marked by disruption and division,
disease, and suffering—have been particularly challenging. Many
of us have endured a deep pain born from isolation and disconnection. Others have had our sense of safety rocked by uncertainty
and loss, forcing us to face our deepest fears and confront our own
mortality.

And yet. From within this collective darkness, I've recognized a
golden thread of light, emanating the hope of new possibility. I've
seen it in the faces of so many of my clients. I've heard it in the
voices of my friends and neighbors.

Because so many of us have come face-to-face with some form
of loss—divorce or break up, bankruptcy, unemployment, retirement, an unwelcome move, a life-threatening illness, the death
of a loved one—we are now embracing life in a new way. We no
longer want to postpone our dreams, our happiness, the "what-

comes-next" chapter of our lives. We've become acutely aware that life doesn't wait. It's finite. And we're ready and willing to do things differently or in a completely new way. Not later, but *now*.

Have you noticed this shift within you? A shift from resignation (*this is just how my life is*) to a reckoning (*maybe it doesn't have to be this way*) to resilience (*I can and will rebuild my life*). It feels like nearly every day now, I speak with people who are crystal clearheaded and resolved that now is the time to start *loving* their lives. Men and women from all over the world sit down with me, either in person or remotely, and courageously voice a deep calling to reevaluate their lives. They acknowledge that the way they've been living for the last ten, twenty, thirty years, or their entire lifetime, is no longer working. They recognize and can admit that their unhealthy habits, repetitive cycles of excess, lack and limitation, competition and comparison, avoidance, denial, or numbing out are no longer serving them. They come to me seeking direction. They ask me to take their hand and lead them through a different door.

And so, I show them a glimpse of heaven.

Because of my ability to tune in to the unseen world, I've been generously granted a sneak peek, and what I happily pass on to my clients and want to share with you now is that heaven is here, now. In this life. And there's no line around the block, no reservation needed.

When I connect with spirits in between the physical and nonphysical worlds, one of the first messages they want to communicate to their living loved ones is that they're okay. *I'm no longer in pain. I'm no longer suffering. I'm not alone. I'm surrounded and being held by others.*

Think: cosmic group hug.

Once I'm able to assure the living that their departed loved ones are in a good place, they tend to want to know what this "good place" is all about. Clients ask me questions like: *Who are they with? What are they doing? Where in the heavens are they?*

Spirits love to answer these questions. I will clairvoyantly see their light bodies jumping up and down and dancing around. Pick me, pick me! The specifics of "who," "what," and "where" vary wildly from spirit to spirit, and some of my favorites include:

· Enjoying a glass of red wine in Tuscany
· Singing in the church choir
· Playing golf at Pebble Beach
· Socializing with friends and family
· Going fishing on a boat and sailing the seas
· Cozying up next to a fireplace while reading their favorite books
· Playing camp counselor, goofing around with a bunch of kids
· Hiking endlessly through the mountains
· Performing in a Broadway musical
· Playing blackjack in Vegas—and winning!
· Taking a joy ride in their dream car
· Skydiving
· Spending hours creating in their art studio
· Sitting peacefully in a garden blooming with their favorite flowers
· Relaxing poolside

In my own meditations, heaven appears to me as a quiet beach at sunset where I imagine myself walking under a sky streaked with yellow, orange, and scarlet as the sun drops into the ocean. As a warm breeze tickles my back, I relax into the feeling of relief and freedom, as well as the promise of some much-deserved rest and restoration.

Spirits use Earthly points of reference like these to paint a familiar and happy picture for their living loved ones as assurance that these spirits are in *their* good place. But remember, heaven is not a place. It's a state of being, a *feeling*. Drinking red wine in Italy feels relaxing. Singing in a church choir feels joyful. Performing onstage feels exhilarating. And soaking up the sun on a tropical beach feels like relief, not unlike when the last day of the school year meets the promise of a long summer.

When I interpret messages from the spirit world, they begin by imprinting images in my mind of their "heaven," and then they quickly accompany their favorite setting with an upsurge of feeling. *Relief. Joy. Connection. Peace.* What I've come to understand is that some of the most beautiful experiences we can have are *felt*, not seen. Perusing pics of your favorite travel destination on VRBO can be thrilling, and yet this removed perspective comes nowhere close to the feeling of digging your toes into the warm sand, right? This is how I understand the concept of heaven. It's more than an idyllic picture. It's the *feeling* associated with the picture, and you are *in your heaven* when you tap into these feelings. Our best vacations are the ones where we feel peaceful, connected, blissed-out, and where our hearts swell with love and gratitude for the people we're with, right? The palm trees are just the backdrop.

Feelings are nebulous things; they are energetic experiences in our body that don't always *feel* quantifiable. And yet, there is a kind of scale we can use to better understand the effect of our feelings on our spiritual well-being. Psychiatrist David R. Hawkins, MD, PhD, and author of the best-selling book *Power vs. Force*, parlayed twenty years of research into a framework called the Map of Consciousness, which I find useful in helping people understand how their emotions and their energy (more on that soon) are intertwined.

Within his framework, "heavenly" feelings are placed at the top of his logarithmic scale (spanning from 0 to 1000) and assigned an energetic frequency. Love, for instance, clocks in at an impressive 500 while fear lands much lower on his scale. I admire Hawkins's work tremendously, and it aligns with what I've observed in my own line of work. We are all energetic beings—the living and the dead—vibrating at varying speeds, and how we *feel* moment to moment determines our energy level, or our frequency. Spirits who have completed their homework feel good; they vibrate at a high energetic frequency. Every day, I channel these spirits who are in their version of heaven, hiking through the mountains or performing in their favorite Broadway musical—I can feel their buzzing energy, too, and it feels amazing. They raise their glass to me, as if to say, I did the work. I earned it and I've arrived.

You can feel the same way—not later, but now—and that's what I'm here to help you do.

What's *Your* Heaven?

Spirits show me different versions of heaven based on their life experiences and their favorite activities and places. What does your heaven look like? Is it a physical location on Earth? Who is with you? What are you wearing? Eating? Doing? Take a moment to visualize this and write it down.

_____

Once you have a solid image in mind, ask yourself: What does "my heaven" *feel* like? Write that down, too.

You Signed Up for This

• • •

At this point you might be wondering: If life can feel so heavenly, why do we sometimes experience just the opposite? I'll level with you—experiencing heaven is a journey. It's not something that happens overnight, nor is it meant to be a final destination. It's something you *feel into* over the course of your time here in Earth School, and along the way, there can be, and most likely will be, some hard turns that don't feel heavenly at all.

But, *why* the struggle?

I meet with people every day who ask me this. They want to know the "why" behind the divorce, the estranged friendship, the job loss, the unexpected medical diagnosis, the loss of a loved one. Maybe you also find yourself asking questions like: *Why me? Why now? Why this?*

The short answer is: whatever is happening in your life—it's happening *for* you, not *to* you. In other words, whatever is haunting you or holding you back is a life assignment that has been custom created for you to tackle and complete. Consider it individualized coursework. Now, before we go any further, I want to pause and underscore that your life is not meant to be a constant struggle. No one deserves hardship. What our departed loved ones, other spirits who guide us from beyond, and angels from the highest realms communicate to me daily is that our challenges are meant to teach us how to become more joyful human beings. Enjoying our lives is our inherent birthright, they say, and we were each born with the tools to work through our struggles with ease and grace. The feeling of suffering is real, but our human attachment to suffering is learned behavior that can be *un*learned.

But I'm jumping ahead. Let's back up. Before we can get to the good stuff, we need to do some work. In my first book, *Spirited*, I walked readers through the delicate process of identifying their biggest struggle and then digging down to its root. As an example, I traced my lifelong struggle with managing my finances back to an early childhood belief that *I am not enough just as I am.* I grew up with a father who demanded attention, and I learned early on to walk on eggshells and play small. As an unconscious coping strategy, it felt safer to attend to Dad's needs rather than to my own, and I was rewarded for being a people pleaser. I felt that part of the way to make others happy was to deny my own worth. As I got older, personal worthiness became conflated with financial worth, and I fell into a habit of financially rescuing other people. I ensured their loyalty by enabling them and trying to fix problems that weren't mine to fix. In my mind, I believed that if people needed my resources, they needed *me* and would, therefore, never abandon me.

When I finally connected these dots, it was like a floodlight flashed on my life. Truly, it was a breakthrough moment. Where I used to automatically listen to that pestering voice in my head that said *You're only valuable to others if you can help them*, I've since learned how to replace that voice with more inspiring messaging that I repeat in my mind like a mantra: **My worth is not defined by my bank account. I do not need to "buy" love.**

In the years since writing *Spirited*, which new readers and longtime clients tell me is still helping them gain clarity about their lives, I've realized that the exercise of naming the obstacle that's in your way and identifying the *why* behind it doesn't go far enough. It's important information, for sure, and yet, there's one more piece to the puzzle. Beyond the why, we must each ask ourselves: *What* does my struggle serve to teach me and *how* will it direct my next step forward?

Once you have your answers, you'll find yourself two steps closer to heaven.

Life Assignments 101

• • •

When I was in my early twenties and just beginning to tap into my ability to connect with spiritual beings, I consumed books like

Journey of Souls by Michael Newton, PhD, *Between Death and Life* by Dolores Cannon, and *Many Lives, Many Masters* by Brian L. Weiss, MD. You may also be familiar with these classics that explore issues of death and the afterlife. (If not, they're well worth a read!) These books fascinated me and introduced me to mind-bending concepts like soul mates and reincarnation that helped me put words to concepts I was beginning to learn from Spirit. They gave me the reference points I needed when I started experiencing things I didn't know how to explain, and I was relieved when I learned that the spirit world also showed itself to others.

Over the years, I've resonated with contemporary works like *Sacred Contracts* by Caroline Myss and *Your Soul's Plan* by Robert Schwartz, which explore the unseen intricacies of our lives. What I find interesting about all of us who study and write about these subjects—medical intuitives, hypnotherapists, psychiatrists, psychologists, and psychic mediums—is that even with our differing backgrounds, experiences, and disciplines, we've arrived at the same basic conclusion: our lives, and the people we meet and the events that happen within them, are not random. Nor are the scales tipped unfairly in any one person's direction. What happens in our lives is by design. And each challenging moment is designed to serve as a teaching or a learning opportunity.

Delivering this news in my readings with clients is usually a low point. You can hear the proverbial pin drop in the room or over the phone line. And when I'm onstage in front of a large audience, this association I make between "struggle" and "learning opportunity" tends to elicit rows upon rows of fallen faces.

I get it. Attributing your struggles to bad luck would feel a whole lot more satisfying. Believe me, there are days when I want to go there, too. In *Sacred Contracts*, Caroline Myss refers to this diversion as "the path of least resistance" and warns that it's actually "more arduous in the long run." That's because whatever is happening, or not happening, in your life, leads *back to you*. Right now you might be thinking, "But, Rebecca, how can it be *my* fault that the housing market is terrible, and I can't sell my house? How could I have stopped the uninsured driver who rear-ended my car? How could I have known that my partner would betray and leave me? Or that the person I loved most would suddenly get sick and die? Why would I bring cancer on *myself*?" The answer: each of these challenging experiences are unfolding to help you learn something, and to pass that learning on to someone else who can equally benefit.

In readings, spirits are eager to reveal that there is no blame to assign because we are each the designers of our lives. There is a plan, an order, and the blueprints were created long ago—before you were born, in fact. That's right, your soul chose specific experiences, relationships, and challenges that would aid your personal growth. In Earth School terms, you chose your own lesson plan. Naturally, the "you" reading this now doesn't remember crafting any such assignment, but my own glimpse of the Other Side confirms it, along with countless spirits who communicate a similar story.

For example, in a recent reading, I felt the energy of a male spirit come through (I know it's masculine energy when I sense a dominant vibration in the room). In my mind's eye, this spirit stepped up to a podium and opened a huge and ancient-looking leather-bound book. I've seen this image many times over the years, and it's become my "sign" that a spirit is referencing their Book of Life, a written record of their choices and lessons, learned and unlearned, in life. As this spirit was flipping through pages, a scene from the popular TV series *Yellowstone* flashed in my mind. I'd been binge-watching the series with my husband, Chris, and I felt an intuitive nudge that the spirit was using this reference to draw a parallel to his own life. To be sure, I asked, *Spirit, show me more.* Next, he flashed an image of Kevin Costner in my mind, the lead actor of the series, whose character has become emotionally hardened over time, cemented by the loss of his wife. As I received this mental picture, I was also delivered a sharp jab to my chest, like when you have heartburn, my "sign" for a heart attack. I put it all together, concluding that this spirit had been similar in nature, emotionally repressed with a guarded heart.

I asked his living son, Jackson, who'd scheduled the reading, if this description fit his father.

"It does, sadly. When my mom died, he closed up, and he was never a very 'open' guy to begin with. Dad came from a long line of military men, and his generation was conditioned to believe you were weak for expressing emotion. As he got older, he just went cold and quiet."

"He died of heartbreak," I said. "And now he's jumping up and down as if to say, *I get it now!* He's showing me his Book of Life, and he's downloading me with a flood of information: He lived his life withdrawn, and when he died, he *remembered* the lesson he'd set up for himself: to live wholeheartedly. Your mom helped him do this, but when she died, he hardened even more and blamed the world for her death and his loss. Now, he wants you to reverse this. He's showing me a lion, my 'sign' for strength, as if to encourage you to recognize strength in vulnerability. Are you still in the military?"

"I retire next year."

"He's saying this is no coincidence. His death and your retirement go hand in hand. They serve as an opening to evolve a dysfunctional family pattern. You can go either way, and Dad is saying: please choose your heart."

In readings like this one, where I'm shown an open Book of Life (or sometimes, a vast library with shelves upon shelves of books), I know the spirit wants to reference their life assignments, and how well they did. When they flash an image of the University of Florida (where I attended as an undergrad) in my mind, this is my "sign" that they've graduated to the next level. Conversely, if they show me an old-fashioned school desk where they're head down with pencil and paper, this tells me that they still have work to do.

Now before we go on, I want to be clear that your goal is not to ace life. It's not about perfection. Making mistakes means you're human, so be human and make a few. Or as my husband likes to say, "Don't keep making the same mistakes; make new ones." Make many. It is through trial and error that we *learn*. Your best effort is what counts.

I'll continue to unpack life assignments in the chapters ahead, but for now, to illustrate how they can play out, I'll take a page out of my own book. For those of you familiar with my personal story, you know that I've written extensively about my father, Shelly, who had the heartbreaking and harrowing experience of finding the lifeless body of his mother, my grandma Babe, who died by suicide. Babe suffered from a lifetime of unaddressed depression, and minus the care she desperately needed, she ultimately chose to resolve her pain by ending her life. Her choice was deeply painful for my dad, who felt abandoned by a mother whose attention to him was limited by her illness. For many years following her death, my dad buried his pain deep inside of him. He refused to acknowledge not only his grief but also the shame he felt at being unable to help someone he loved, who may not have been able to be helped at all. In doing so, he also positioned himself far from help. My two brothers and I were never allowed to talk about what happened to our grandmother. The topic was taboo, and so we all silently, and quite independently, suffered through what was a shared sense of loss and confusion. Like his own mother, Dad chose to check out from our family's collective experience—from us. But isolation came at a cost: with time, his unresolved pain transitioned into a debilitating depression that resulted in his own suicide.

I know, it's a lot.

But it didn't have to be this way.

From the perspective of Earth School, Dad's "assignment" was to distinguish his mother's pain from his own. The kid in him felt betrayed, but Grandma Babe's decision to end her life wasn't a betrayal of anyone but herself. If Dad could have reconciled that her death was not his fault, he may have found his way to forgiving her and he may have forgiven himself. He may also have cultivated some compassion for her illness, and even come to accept the things he couldn't control or even fully understand. Instead, he became even more entrenched in his hurt, trapped by it until it engulfed him. In dreams and in deep meditation, I've "seen" my dad hunched over a school desk. Not only has he had to work hard to finish his assignment in spirit form by resolving his feelings around his mom's death, but because of the way he left his own life, he also must now additionally grapple with the legacy of pain and suffering he created for his living loved ones.

I could have gone down the same road as Dad, and in fact, I almost did. When my family's history of depression came to claim me, I was in college, struggling to find my way as a new adult living away from home for the first time. My internal battle began to manifest in the kitchen, where I unconsciously used food to numb the pain. A chance encounter with a therapist who recommended journaling changed everything for me. Through a process called automatic writing, combined with my developing gifts as a medium, my grandma Babe reached out her etheric hand and reconnected with me on the page. For a year and a half, she spoke to me. I interpreted her words and guidance through my pen as she urged me to address my genetic predisposition to depression and make choices that were different from what she did. Alongside her loving guidance, continued therapy, nutritional counseling, supervised temporary medication, and loving support from family and friends, I was saved from my dangerous low. And because I faced my pain and did the hard work, I was able to disrupt an unhealthy family cycle.

No One Gets a Pass

• • •

The stakes are high for incomplete assignments because you aren't the only person impacted by them. In my family, our father's suicide devastated us. In addition to what we were already tackling in our own lives, Dad's unfinished work presented us with an "extra" assignment of picking up where he left off—which included confronting our guilt and regrets and forgiving him as well as ourselves.

My brothers and I have all approached this work in our own ways. I grieved deeply—as any daughter would—but my professional and personal access to higher realms gave me a unique perspective that brought me peace. I understood that my dad hadn't chosen to abandon *us*; his failure to embrace his opportunity to learn from his mom's mental illness had caused him to abandon *himself* and ultimately, perpetuate the cycle. But, even for me, this recognition took time. Years, in fact. Today, my intention and hope is that my family is creating a new legacy rooted in mental health and that a new cycle of resilience has ripple effects on many generations to come.

Seizing the Opportunity

• • •

Without realizing it, many of us are currently working through assignments left behind by our parents, grandparents, and generations that came before us. In some families, the ingrained patterns are subtle and go undetected, like the father who was overly critical of his son, justifying it as "tough love." Decades later, this boy grows up to become a father with the same tendencies, expecting his son to "man up," rather than connect with his authenticity and vulnerability. Or there's the mother who emotionally manipulates her daughter as a way to get her own needs met. *"If you really love me, you will . . ."* After a lifetime of being manipulated, the daughter becomes a mother who unconsciously carries forward the same pattern with her children. (In my family, we call this Jewish guilt.) A more dangerous form of manipulation is a narcissistic parent (who is probably a product of a narcissistic parent) who tends to play the victim role, expecting the world to revolve around them and cater to their needs. Gone unchecked, this behavior is likely to show up in their children, who carry forward the same mentality.

Another common intergenerational thread I see is a scarcity mindset. Many of us had grandparents or great-grandparents who lived through the Great Depression and who adopted the mindset that there's never enough to go around. This type of thinking is pervasive and is unconsciously passed down through so many families who believe that they, too, will always suffer from lack.

In other families, inherited mistakes and unfinished work are harder to miss. Like the three generations of domestic abuse, where a husband assaults his wife, just as his father and grandfather once did theirs. Or the anti-Semitic or racist parents who fail to choose education over ignorance and pass their hateful views to their children. Or the addictions that, left unaddressed, can plague generation after generation, ruining lives in the process.

Understand that in all these true-life stories, there is something bigger at play than "bad luck," being in the wrong place, in the wrong family, or inheriting bad genes. Rather, there is an intergenerational lesson, a group assignment that's overdue, and if this unfinished work is not addressed, then it will inadvertently be passed down to the next generation. This spiritual hand-me-down is common throughout most family lines, which is why it comes up with high frequency in my readings.

In nearly every reading I do, spirits come through to make amends for their regrettable actions, or inactions, in life. They offer specifics, like in the examples above, finally realizing the impact their choices had on the safety and happiness of their family. They express regret over missed opportunities and wrong turns and urge their own children to *not* live or lead by their example. They might mention how careless and reckless they were with money, for example, and implore their living loved ones to "spend smarter." The examples are many, but the takeaway is the same: *break the cycle and do it differently.*

Easier said than done, which is why so many of these tough assignments do go unfinished. But for those of us who can bravely embrace the learning and healing opportunity within the hard work, the rewards are great.

Which is exactly what my husband, Chris, and his father, a retired psychiatrist, are experiencing now. For the better part of his adult life, Chris and his dad have had a challenging relationship, both holding on to old resentments. As Chris explained it to me, "It's hard to get close to Dad because he's self-righteous, hypercritical, and he never admits to being wrong, which means—it's never his fault; it's my fault." But when Chris's dad started to lose his battle with Parkinson's disease at the age of eighty-one, Chris decided, *enough is enough.* He recognized that time to reconcile with his dad was short. In Earth School terms, it was 8:00 P.M. on Sunday night and they both still had a lot of unfinished work to do. So, Chris extended an invitation to connect.

Chris credits the very insights we're discussing here for what happened next. He directly shared the idea of life assignments with his dad, and the consequences of skipping Earth School. Chris said to his dad pointedly, "I don't want you to die with regrets, and I certainly don't want that to happen to me, so let's have this conversation now while we have the chance." Chris was optimistic: "I think we can still clean this up; we can still have a relationship." And he joked, "Plus, you really don't want to relive this fight with me in the next life, do you?"

To Chris's surprise, his dad laughed and lightened. He relaxed and opened up for the first time in years.

"It was the simplicity of the 'life assignments' idea that finally seemed to cut through," Chris told me. "I guess because talking about his life from a zoomed-out perspective meant that we didn't have to dive back into the details of who did what to whom in the past. It was a less confrontational approach."

Chris smiled as he continued, "I could see it in his face. It's like there was finally a crack in the dam, and in that moment, he became willing to question himself. He stepped back and recognized that his need to be right and justify his actions had kept him stuck in this endless cycle where he was at odds with others, and that this 'assignment' of his was still unfinished and it would stay unfinished until he shifted his behavior and broke the cycle." Chris leaned forward with tears in his eyes. "Becky, he told me he loved me for the first time in *twenty-five years*."

After their transformational talk, Chris's dad started making amends everywhere! He reached out to his partner, some of his oldest friends, and finally, Chris's brother, John. "He's been critical of my brother since we were both kids," Chris said, "and Dad actually apologized for that. An apology from a man who has never been able to bring himself to admit he's done anything wrong. *That* was a true reckoning."

At the near-term end of his life, Chris's dad is finally tackling his assignments—to learn humility and acceptance of other people's differences. And the benefits of this real-time life review aren't exclusive to him. Chris said that their conversation brought some of his own assignments to light.

"Like what?" I asked.

"I'm still learning how to be compassionate toward Dad and have a relationship with him without giving up what I need from the relationship," Chris said.

"So do you think that *your* lesson in this is to learn how to set healthy boundaries that honor your worth and respect your needs despite how others treat you?" I suggested.

"That sounds about right," Chris reflected. "I'm still thinking it through, what it means for me. Initially, I thought I was having the conversation *for* Dad, but now I can see that it was for me, too. We waited long enough, but I think I just got ahead of regrets that I may have had if Dad had died without a reconciliation. In clearing up a struggle that has weighed me down for most of my life, I feel ... *different*. More gratitude for the relationship I do have with him. Free of old resentment and grudges." Chris took in a deep breath and let it out slowly. He smiled. "I feel relief."

Relief. The *feeling* of heaven.

Let's Get to Work

• • •

As a spiritual medium, I meet upward of five thousand people a year who are seeking hope, insight, and answers to their biggest questions. As you might guess, many arrive with a lot of queries about the afterlife, but more than that, what they are seeking is guidance on how to *live*. They ask me: How do I stop repeating the same patterns? How can I finally let go of what pains me, and move on with my life?

Over the past year, I have clairvoyantly seen so many of my clients standing at a crossroads where they are being presented with the choice to stay right where they are, in effect postponing their homework for another day, or to take a courageous step forward and complete the assignment at hand. More than ever before, people are eager to put pencil to paper.

My sense is that you're also at a crossroads. Are you up for the task at hand?

I thought so. Let's get to work.

CHAPTER 2

Progress Report

. . .

If you feel like you're living your life passively, on autopilot, or that you're stuck in a struggle and life is not flowing with ease and joy—these are cues that you have unfinished work to do. You might be wondering what the assignment is. But before you can identify the work you still have to complete, you must first name the struggle, the "Why is this happening?" or the "Why is this *not* happening in my life?" I know I said that naming your struggle doesn't go far enough, but it is the starting point, and it is always where I begin in my readings.

On the Other Side, this reflective process is called the "life review." After spirits cross over, they look back at their lives, not unlike the scene from in the 1990s comedy *Defending Your Life* with Albert Brooks and Meryl Streep. In deep meditation and in readings, spirits have shown me a similar review process to that depicted in the movie, but instead of a stark and serious environment, they describe to me—by flashing a series of images into my mind—a variety of settings most conducive to the spirit's comfort level, such as sitting around a campfire or in a beautiful garden. Some gather in a temple-like sanctuary. Others plop down on a cushy couch, like in a therapist's office. Very few spirits choose the intensity of a courtroom to review their lives. I mean, would you choose to sit in a trial box when you could review your life in a reclining beach chair?

In the spirit's chosen setting, they are escorted by a loving guide and joined by their review board, a group generally made up of three to eight senior-level spirits, sometimes referred to as directors, judges, and teachers who were human once and have risen in the ranks to "master elder" status. By way of meditation, hypnotherapy, and the countless readings I've done with spirits, my understanding is that we each have a Council of Elders on the Other Side. These beings have paid their dues by tackling and passing their own life lessons when they were alive—sometimes over several lifetimes—which gives them the experience and wisdom to support the deceased in looking back at their own lives.

In the spirit world, all council members, ranging in personality, skill sets, and expertise, share a vested interest in the spirit they're advising. They assemble around the deceased with love and compassion, creating an openhearted and safe space. They take a neutral stance, withholding critical judgment and yet exercising discernment as they encourage the spirit to take an honest self-inventory of the accumulation of their thoughts, words, actions, and reactions throughout their lifetimes. In *Journey of Souls*, Michael Newton shares detailed accounts of his subjects' experiences under hypnosis, describing the council as "gentle but probing. Imagine your favorite elementary school teacher and you have the idea. Think of a firm but concerned entity who knows all about your learning habits, your strong and weak points, and your fears, and who was always ready to work with you as long as you continue to try." Like every good teacher, coach, mentor, or therapist, each council member will ask the spirit thought-provoking questions leading to the spirit's own answers and truth, because it is the spirit who must ultimately play both judge and jury. Did I pass the tests in front of me, or did I fall short of completing my homework? Did I sincerely try to do and be better, after learning from my mistakes? Did I honor myself, honor others, and live a life of integrity?

The spirit, along with the council, seek to answer these questions by illuminating on a white screen what I've termed "sliding door moments," specific times in our lives where we were presented with a choice: Door A or Door B? Opportunity 1 or Opportunity 2? In the prebirth planning stage, our souls consider our choices and options. And while there is a best-case scenario or a Door A, it's not the only door in Earth School. Though Door A tends to open easily because it leads us forward with grace and ease toward learning and advancement, we don't always choose it. Why? Because we don't want to. We don't feel like it. Because we think Door B might be better. Or Door C better yet. Because we're humans who like to exercise our free will!

With each door that we open, we're presented with a different set of experiences that offer us the opportunity to learn the same important lesson. However, with each door you pass, you're making your life a little bit more difficult, because the alternative doors get harder and harder to open. They create resistance to the natural flow of your life, and even with a good shove, they don't open all the way, or worse, they lead you right back to where you started. As

Spirit often reminds me: you can learn your life lessons through pain and struggle, or through grace, ease, and joy. The choice is yours. Will you choose the door that is the straight shot to where you're meant to go, or the one that creates a detour and delay?

My stepdaughter Hannah recently served to remind me how a sliding door moment can play out. Like many sixteen-year-olds, Hannah couldn't wait to turn her learner's permit into a driver's license. Our family celebrated her "ticket to freedom"—more independence for her, less carpooling for us. We were all on a high until a few weeks later, when she got her first speeding ticket. I gently suggested to Hannah that this was Spirit's way of saying: take it easy and slow down. And just as the rest of the teenagers in my house react to my otherworldly guidance, my cautionary line fell on deaf ears. Back on the road after paying off her ticket and finishing her first round of traffic school, Hannah rear-ended a truck. Thankfully no one was hurt, but both vehicles were damaged, and on top of her speeding ticket, our insurance rate suffered. Once again, I suggested that this was a nudge from Spirit that she ought to "learn her lesson" before something else happened. Believing in the pattern of three, I worried for her. In my line of work, the number three represents Divine perfection, and so when I want Spirit to validate a hunch or underscore a point, I will say: show me evidence in threes. Hannah had already had two accidents, and now, I feared a third was waiting right around the corner. And sure enough, a few months later she ran smack into another car. It was a significant crash and completely her fault. Again, no one was seriously hurt, but our car was totaled, Hannah's driving record was wrecked, and her personal freedom was retracted.

Even though I was frustrated with Hannah's choices, I respect that we each get to pick our doors. We each get to choose our own adventure, even if it gets us in a wreck and totals the family car. Unfortunately, some of us total our lives before we finally step forward and account for our choices. Better late than never, but for Hannah's sake, I hoped and prayed for *sooner rather than later*. I'm happy to report that in Hannah's case, her detour served a purpose.

While on a parental-imposed suspension from driving, Hannah returned to her childhood pastime and love of horseback riding and grooming. She sulked about it at first, but within a couple of weeks, we noticed a profound and positive shift in her mental and emotional health. She became more serious about her schoolwork, showed trust in a bigger picture, and she was in less of a rush to get to the next place in her life. It was clear to us—and to her—that she was finally learning her lesson, though it certainly didn't happen the easy way.

More on Doors

We each come into our lives with a loose script that outlines the events, relationships, and challenges that will likely unfold within our lifetime, and that present us with the greatest opportunities to learn important lessons. Each script contains a set of "doors," so to speak, that allow us to either advance or stall our progress. Where Door A may be the better choice because it leads toward growth with ease and efficiency, we may exercise our right to free will and choose Door B or Door C, and on and on. The doors and the opportunities are endless.

When you choose the harder door and postpone the lesson being presented to you, it returns as a new door. A new opportunity to learn the same lesson. And the question is: Will you select the door that easily opens the next time, or will you once again try the door that pushes back? The choice is yours.

If you understand your options, wouldn't you prefer to select the door of least resistance? Wouldn't you rather tackle your work sooner than later? If you opt to postpone your assignments until the afterlife, that is your choice, although I feel it is my obligation to give you a preview of what awaits you in the next—yet another set of doors.

In the afterlife scenario, Door A leads you back to Earth School to finish your work, and Door B allows you to stay on the Other Side and let your living loved ones pick up where you left off. This is the generational hand-me-down that I referenced earlier. Any work you leave unfinished is assigned down the line, typically to your next of kin. While this may sound like the preferable option (what a deal, someone else finishing my work!), you're not off the hook. If you opt for Door B, you will be held responsible for assisting your loved one, and I don't think I have to point out the obvious here—the dead coaching the living is fraught with less-than-ideal communication lines and practical meeting spots. Add to that, before a spirit can offer assistance, they must first reconcile their own death. Depending on the spirit, this can take a long time, especially when you consider that time is a relative construct after death. Spirits often communicate that "time" for them is not linear like it is here on Earth, but circular and sometimes expansive, especially for spirits who have died tragically or by making poor choices that led to their death. These spirits have significant healing to do before they can be of any help to the living.

In readings with spirits who died by suicide, for example, I will typically "see" them in a hospital ICU bed where they are receiving light energy transfusions that help to heal and repair them on a deep, soul level. The mental image I've received from the Other Side looks a lot like being hooked up to an IV that's pumping essential vitamins, minerals, and nutrients back into the body, and in this case, the etheric body. Spirits have also compared their recovery process to charging a cell phone battery that's been worn down to a low- or no-percent battery. Life has a way of beating us down and depleting us on physical, mental, and emotional levels, and some spirits arrive on the Other Side with a battery blinking in the red, in desperate need for restoration. My grandma Babe had been gone for ten years before she was able to reach out and help guide me out of my depression. My father had been gone for nearly a year before I started having clear visitations from him. The bottom line is that whoever you are, you cannot escape the work. You pick up where you left off, and it takes effort in whatever realm you choose to complete it.

Back for More

When I said that you can "come back" and tackle unfinished work in Earth School, yes, I was referring to the concept of reincarnation. My perspective on this is not grounded in any religious tradition or context—rather, it's the result of countless communications I've received from spirits. I've been shown that when we leave Earth School with unfinished work to do, it is our responsibility to make it right, to learn the intended lesson. Over the years, spirits have relayed to me that the most efficient way to do this is to reincarnate into a physical body because we can finish our work faster in the environment in which it was originally started. Kind of like, if it happened in Vegas, fix it in Vegas.

This idea of carrying our own unfinished business, as well as any incomplete assignments handed down through our ancestral lines over lifetimes, is central to the idea of "karma." Karma is a key concept in the Hindu, Jain, Buddhist, and Sikh religions. Your karma is recorded in your Book of Life, also referred to in my spiritual circles as the "cosmic tally book," and one that makes note of our intentions and actions in life with the understanding that how we show up day to day has a cause and effect, and in the end, each negative must be balanced with a positive in order to heal and elevate our souls.

As an example, if you had a bad habit of lying, scamming, or stealing from others and left this lifetime without making things right with yourself, and with those you harmed or violated, your soul would be better served to heal this cycle by reincarnating back into a body where you can clean up your mess. This next go-round, you may sign up to be on the receiving end of someone who lies to you, and by playing an opposing role, you learn empathy and grow compassion. Or, using the same scenario, you may choose to return as an advocate or a defender of people who are hurt or violated, and by doing so you redeem your past by making things right this time.

For those souls who don't have a lot of karma to balance because they completed or put forth their best effort to complete their assignments on time, their decision to reincarnate may be motivated by a desire to serve others. These generous, advanced souls often act as mentors, teachers, coaches, and guides to the living. We all know people like this, whether we identify them this way or not, who are on assignment to help us learn, grow, and fulfill our greatest potential. We'll explore the work of these advanced souls later, but for now, look around at the people in your life. Can you identify who may be serving that role? It's not by coincidence. These "helpers" didn't just happen into your life; they are here by design.

Stories from Beyond

• • •

The ability I have as a medium helps me to name the thing that's weighing down a client—mentally, emotionally, spiritually, or physically—and preventing them from moving forward. As an example, when I was reading my client Kim, the spirit of her grandmother forcefully came through. She projected her energy into my upper back, which felt like an electric shock that traveled down to my knee. She followed this by flashing an image in my mind of a man standing by Kim's side. I intuitively knew that Grandma was referencing Kim's current relationship with her husband, and this was coupled with a feeling in my stomach of dread and disappointment. This is typically how a spirit will communicate with me, through all my senses. They will throw a bunch of things at me at once—images, sounds, feelings, and insights—and it is my job to put them together into a clear and accurate narrative for the living. In this case, my read on the situation was that Kim was struggling with back pain, and maybe knee pain, as a result of something else going on in her life, something that had either been unaddressed or not properly attended to. The pain was her cue to finally attend to the deeper struggle. I had a strong hunch that it was tied to her marriage, so I just asked her, "Are you struggling in your marriage?"

Kim nodded, and I sensed her disappointment and doubt in her husband.

"Your grandmother is saying 'enough is enough.' Does that make sense to you?"

Kim drew in a sharp breath. "Oh my God, yes. I think he's lying to me, but I've been doubting myself until just this morning I wrote those exact words in my journal—*enough is enough*."

"This is your validation that your grandmother can hear you and she is acting as your guide from the Other Side. She wants you to trust your knowing. He's gaslighting you," I said as Grandma flashed a propane tank in my mind's eye, "and she's only telling you what you already know."

Kim laughed. "She never sugarcoated anything. Always direct and to the point."

"You're ready to confront the truth about your marriage," I said, "or she wouldn't be this direct with you now. My sense is that once you begin trusting yourself again and start standing up for yourself, your back will stop hurting. She's literally showing me a strong spine. Do you see the connection?"

"I do," Kim said. She tearfully shared that she didn't feel supported in her marriage and that over the years, she'd become resentful of her husband. "But I was determined to make it work," she said. "It's not my personality to walk away and honestly, I've been afraid to end it and move forward without him, so I think I've been making excuses for him and looking the other way when I know he hasn't been truthful with me."

"Think of it this way," I said. "Your pain is acting like a messenger, trying to get your attention. There's an important lesson here for you to learn. It's as if your back is saying—stand up tall and honor yourself. Take the next step forward, and when in doubt, call on your grandmother. She is here to help you, but remember: no one knows you better than you know yourself. She is simply acting as a flashlight, illuminating for you what you already know is there, but that you may have buried or chosen to look away from. Grandma is nudging you to turn on the lights."

Homework

LIFE REVIEW: TURN ON THE LIGHTS

In readings, I intuitively feel a strong wave of compassion, empathy, and forgiveness emanate from the Council of Elders when I'm offered a glimpse into a spirit's review process. It's delicate work that requires honesty and kindness, so as you courageously complete the following life review in real time, I encourage you to also reserve judgment and self-blame and instead practice self-compassion.

To help you better see and uncover your truths, start by getting quiet and then asking:

Is there anything in my life that feels difficult, unresolved, or off track? What is not serving me well? What is draining me or holding me back from the life I want?

Give yourself a few minutes of quiet, focused attention and let images of people, specific events, and circumstances come to mind. Include "numbing" practices like indulging in food and drink, recreational drugs, shopping, social media, TV, excessive exercise, or long hours at work that may point to a deeper struggle. Again, try not to edit, judge, or critique what comes to mind. Let it surface.

Most of us wrestle with many hard things, and there's a lesson to be learned from every one of them—but not all at once. What I've come to understand through my own trial and error, and with a helpful download of guidance from Spirit, is that when we fracture and divide our energy and attention by attempting to focus on everything at the same time, not only can we become anxious and overwhelmed, paralyzed about taking action or desperately motivated to take the wrong action, but also we can lose perspective of what a particular struggle is meant to teach us. As Gary Keller succinctly writes in his book, *The One Thing: The Surprisingly Simple Truth Behind Extraordinary Results*, "When you give your ONE Thing your most emphatic 'Yes!' and vigorously say 'No!' to the rest, extraordinary results become possible."

So, for the purpose of this exercise, focus on the one struggle in your life today that rises to the top of your awareness. Name that struggle.

Next, we're going to pivot our exploration from the *thinking* mind and into our *feeling* hearts, where our deepest knowing resides. When we set the intention to move solely out of our head and drop into our heart, we create *coherence*, which is "the state when the heart, mind and emotions are in energetic alignment and cooperation," explains HeartMath Institute Research director Dr. Rollin McCraty. As it relates to self-exploration, when our intellect and instinct are cooperating and honored in equal measure is when we uncover the truth.

Get out of your MIND ⇨ *and into the HEART of your struggle.*

You've just named your struggle. Now, can you assign a *feeling* to your struggle? Ask your heart, *How do I feel in relation to my struggle?* Remember, difficult feelings are important clues that can point you toward healing and growth. When you feel unsettled, consider it a nudge from your heart. Feel into it first, ask questions later.

Resentment Anger Disappointment
Bitterness **Anxiety** Insecurity
Hurt Loneliness
Powerlessness Distrust and doubt
Desperation **Competition**
Disrespect
Overwhelm Frustration
Burnout Fatigue **Fear**
Guilt
Shame

Not exactly a feel-good list, is it? And yet, a feeling or two (or three!) may ring true to you because most of us wrestle with a handful of them depending on the day. Having "off" days, low-down moods, even shitty weeks, or a couple of bad years is par for the course. It's the price of admission to Earth School. So, don't beat yourself up for being a human who sometimes feels bad. What you do want to pay attention to are these feelings. From the word cloud provided, are there any that repeat or *spin* with regularity? Are there feelings from this list that wait for you upon waking in the morning? Or that follow you through-out the day, impacting your mood and influencing your rela-tionships and interactions with others? Pay attention to those emotions. At the height of my financial struggle, I was plagued by feelings of powerlessness that, in turn, created resentment that I projected onto others as blame. This was my emotional spin cycle, and it was a hellish ride.

The Energetic Hand-Me-Down

• • •

Where spirits describe heaven as the *feeling of* connection, ease, joy, freedom, and safety, they conversely describe hell not as a physical pit of volcanic lava, but as being stuck in a painful spin cycle of hurt and negative feelings in this lifetime. So often in readings, spirits will impress feelings into my emotional body to commu-nicate that they were in a "living hell" on Earth, stuck in a cycle of worry, resentment, and fear. I can sometimes "see" a family pat-tern of these feelings that travel across generations, illustrated as a squiggly through line of low energy that looks not unlike the pulses and plateaus produced from an electrocardiogram heart sensor. Dr. Hawkins parks these low vibrational feelings under 200 on his scale. Fear, specifically, clocks in at 100 and shame occupies the very bottom of the scale at 20. Unfortunately, too many of us regularly vibrate at these lower levels.

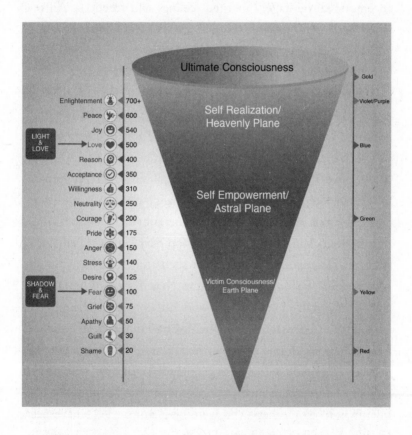

Not only do fear and shame feel bad pulsing through our bodies, but these feelings also emit energy that can be felt and subconsciously replicated by those around us. It's not uncommon to pick up on and be influenced by somebody's bad mood, right? Well, it goes further than impacting the people in our homes, workspaces, and communities. Our feelings extend backward and forward through our lineage. "I come from a long line of worriers," my friend Cindy often says. "People in my family get loud, angry, and fight," confides Heather, a colleague of mine. We each have an emotional heritage. Inherited feelings and reactions. Anyone who's part of the tribe is familiar with "Jewish motherly guilt," which is well intentioned but equally disempowering. I've come to understand that this is more than a custom or a tradition.

The emerging science of epigenetics show us that family traits can be passed down in our DNA. Specifically, epigeneticists study inherited changes in gene expression. The environment we live in—social, cultural, geographic, etc.—influences the expression of our genes. So, too, does our lived experience. Deeply impactful events, like trauma, can actually change our DNA, and those changes get passed down to future generations.

Inherited changes in gene expression have been studied extensively in Holocaust survivors. One such study conducted at the Mount Sinai School of Medicine in New York City found that adult children of Holocaust survivors had epigenetic changes to a gene linked to cortisol, a hormone involved in the stress response. Researchers also found a distinctive pattern of DNA methylation, another epigenetic marker. They concluded that both parents and unborn children were affected on a genetic level. In other research, infants born to mothers who were pregnant on 9/11 have been found to have impacted cortisol levels, which were associated with the presence of maternal PTSD."

"Collective trauma" isn't a term usually applied to single-family dynamics, and yet, what I hear from spirits time and again is that we hold *energetic* remnants of trauma in our DNA that have been passed down through our generational lines. The energetic remnants of fear or distrust, for example, can be at the heart of our present-day struggle, even if it didn't originate with us and will often stand in the way of our ability to create the life we desire. I've observed many clients achieve some level of freedom from their struggle only to slip backward because of energetic programming that was hardwired into their bodies many generations back.

But it doesn't have to stay that way.

"The groundbreaking discovery of epigenetics tells a new story about our ability to change," writes Dr. Nicole LePera in her book, *How to Do the Work.* Through my own line of work, spirits will often encourage their living loved ones to "wake up" and become consciously aware of hereditary *feelings* that may be bumping around in their genes and causing them pain in the present, prompting them to transcend old programming. And in fact, exciting new science confirms that we can affect the expression of our DNA by changing our daily thought and feeling patterns. Once we become aware that a certain person, situation, or environment has a negative effect on our lives, we can make conscious changes to protect ourselves from such stressors. In other words, while we don't have control over what was passed down to us, if we consciously shift our energy into higher frequencies in the present day, we can evolve old programming born out of trauma and fear and affect how our genes are expressed down the ancestral line. In fact, once we begin this work on ourselves, we automatically, and often unconsciously, create an opportunity for our children to heal their own DNA and lineage. After all, our children chose us because they recognized an energetic match to their own energy, a family, or even a single family member that would help them heal deep wounds on both a genetic and soul level.

"Our ancestors exist in our genes, and also in our patterns, emotions, traumas, and the way that we think and feel. These traits affect our everyday lives in both negative and positive ways, but when we heal hereditary wounds in ourselves, we can transform energetic patterns with a vibrational shift in the entire ancestral line and seven generations in the future," teaches Shamanic Energy Healer (and my sister-in-law) Ariela HaLevi.

Did you get that? We can transform inherited feelings and patterns by simply shifting our energy. Sounds like a great way to make a dent in our homework, doesn't it?

Feelings = Vibration

• • •

Think about your own family for a minute. Is there a *feeling* that runs throughout? A feeling that has simply become a way your family describes itself, almost like a personality trait? *We're worriers. We rage. We play it safe. We're "judgy."* Many families do this, typically unconsciously, and now you are being called to understand how your feelings, and the energy they emit, create both your day-to-day reality and your family legacy.

At the cellular level, human life is fueled by energy. When we allow worry, resentment, and fear to vibrate within our bodies, we both emit and attract that energetic vibration back to us. The level and quality of our energy determines the people who are in our lives and heavily influences our life events. Simply, our energetic vibration determines our heaven or hell. Now, don't freak. Our feelings change minute to minute, which means our vibration does, too, and in the pages ahead, I'll help to guide you up the Hawkins scale until you're vibrating as close to 1000 as you can get, the frequency of unconditional love and ultimate consciousness, the energy of heaven. For now, trust that any low-level feelings you're wrestling with can serve to point you toward unresolved work, an important life lesson that *you* set up to learn to aid your own growth and to heal the generations behind and in front of you.

Every week, I meet with hundreds of people who deeply desire my guidance alongside pointed direction from enlightened spirits, and what I hear myself saying on repeat is: *your* feelings are your best guide. Listen to them. Your feelings, and especially the low-level ones that nudge and nag you, want to be heard. Imagine your feelings are out on a football field with a bullhorn, shouting: *Hey, you in the stands, pay attention to me!* Your feelings serve to alert you to something important that needs your attention. An important clue. And the guidance I receive from the Other Side is that you will gain tremendous new insight into your life when you listen.

All the Feels

• • •

The following Let It Be visualization exercise that I've adapted from Dr. Hawkins's *Letting Go: The Pathway of Surrender* is designed to help you bring up feelings and name them in a safe and loving way. It's important to create space to do this work because many of us tend to dismiss, deny, power through, or project our hard feelings onto others. In *Rising Strong*, Brené Brown provides insight behind this: "Emotion can feel terrible, even physically overwhelming. We can feel exposed, at risk, and uncertain in the midst of emotion. Our instinct is to run from pain. In fact, most of us were never taught how to hold discomfort, sit with it, communicate it, only how to discharge or dump it, or to pretend that it's not happening." I recognize this in people every day who come to me after bypassing their pain for months, years, sometimes even entire lifetimes, because they're afraid to *go there*. I get it. I relate to running and hiding. In my early days of mediumship work, I resonated with the popular "shine love and light on it" philosophy, which I've since come to understand is just a form of spiritual bypass, a term coined by transpersonal psychotherapist John Welwood, who wrote extensively about it in his book: *Toward a Psychology of Awakening*. As Welwood defines it, spiritual bypassing is the "tendency to use spiritual ideas and practices to sidestep or avoid facing unresolved emotional issues, psychological wounds, and unfinished developmental tasks." Spiritual bypassing is a defense mechanism and a method of hiding behind spirituality or spiritual practices, where you *shine love and light*, rather than acknowledge and embrace your true feelings and your shadow side. In other words: avoiding the dark stuff. And the problem with this strategy is that eventually, if not immediately around the next corner, your rage, depression, or despair will resurface. It will return to impede your way. The fastest route to feeling better, then, is to face your pain head-on. As I often say: in order to heal it, you have to feel it.

I want to underscore that your difficult feelings do not define you, they aren't *you*, they aren't permanent, nor should they be used to determine the quality or "success" of your life. Your feelings are just information. Information that you're going to use in the pages ahead to take one step closer to heaven. You see, it's only when we begin to shift our feelings from the inside out that our external circumstances can change in reflection. We all have it within us to turn our pain into something beautiful, something heavenly. And the doorway is through the heart.

Exercise

····

Let It Be Visualization

Start by taking three deep, cleansing breaths to center and ground you into the present moment. With your intention and attention, breathe down into your heart center and as you do, ask your spirit guides and your departed loved ones to help you bring your feelings forth. Say: *Thank you for helping me to step out of my head and into my heart. Thank you for allowing me the stillness I need to open and receive guidance, right here, right now.*

Once you're still, invite your feelings to come forward. With curiosity, ask: *What am I feeling?* Take your time and, eventually, dial into the **one** feeling that feels most relevant in the moment. When you're ready, name the feeling that steps forward and then, sit with it. Try not to judge it or make it different. Just be with it. Acknowledge its energy and, if you can, conjure gratitude for the feeling. Smile at it. Thank it for coming forward and showing itself at this time to help you understand the heart of your struggle.

Pay attention to where you feel it in your body and let it rest there, or if you feel it everywhere, let it flow through you. If the feeling is painful, breathe into it. Inhale deeply. Exhale with intention. If the feeling generates thoughts, which is highly likely, return to and focus on your breath. Turn down your thoughts as much as you can and allow the *feeling* to be. Let it be.

 Bonus Material! For an audible version of this exercise, use the QR code at the back of the book.

Name Your Feeling

• • •

If you haven't already, name your feeling. Just one. The one that pushes against you the most and has risen to the surface right now. Can you bravely name it?

Once you've named your *feeling*, write it down or hold it in your mind. Just be mindful of clutching it too tightly. If you give your feeling extra attention by self-identifying with it—*I* AM afraid, *I* AM disconnected, *I* AM insecure, the feeling will magnify and expand, creating even more of that low-level energy within your body. Not only will this reinforce the feeling, but it will also energetically emanate outward and act like a boomerang back to you, because emotion is energy in motion. In the chapters ahead, I will guide you to shift the feeling, but for now, loosen your grip. Observe it as if it's resting in the palm of your hand. For a little extra credit, check out the Divinely Held Visualization on the next page.

Extra Credit

Divinely Held

Close your eyes. Take several deep inhales and exhales. Imagine your hurt feeling in the open palm of your hand. Observe it. Acknowledge it. Now, mentally invite your spirit guides and deceased loved ones to place their hands over your own and hold your feeling in love and compassion, just like you would cradle or comfort a child or a favorite pet. Allow your heart to swell with love and gratitude for this feeling, recognizing it as important information to help free you of your struggle. Imagine a bright white light growing between your hands, holding your feeling in Divine light.

The Relationship Connection

• • •

Struggle ⇨ Feeling ⇨ Relationship

Your last bit of work to do in this chapter is to draw one more line of connection between your *struggle*, your *feeling,* and a *relationship.* Can you assign your *feeling* to one of the following relationships?

Relationship with *Spirit*

Relationship with *Self*

Relationship with *Others*

What spirits have shown me is that our life assignments are always connected to one or more of these relationships. As examples, feelings of shame are most connected to your relationship with *Self*. Resentments and anger are often tied to relationships with *Others*. And feelings of disconnection point to our relationship with *Spirit*, the biggest and brightest energy source.

When departed spirits share their regrets for what they didn't get to do on Earth, they rarely reference bucket list experiences like going to Hawaii or buying a convertible. Rather, they voice regrets over unresolved or unfinished relationships. Spirits share sentiments like the ones below in every single one of my readings:

- I feel deep remorse for not being more present and showing up for the important people in my life.
- I feel anguish that I prioritized my work over spending time with my child.
- I feel guilty that I didn't fully appreciate and tell my parents how much I loved them.
- I feel deep regret that I didn't trust people, myself, and life more.
- I feel frustrated that I was too proud to apologize to my partner.
- I feel ashamed that I undervalued the importance of making true connections with people.

Some of our hardest work is to learn how to be in relationship— with ourselves, with the people in our lives, and with the world, seen and unseen. We cannot opt for independent study hall; we can only truly learn our most important life lessons through our relationships. People come to me every day who are confused, angry, or suffering from a personal relationship that's fraught with difficulty—and they don't know why. What I'm able to do for my clients, and what I want to teach you, is to identify why you're struggling with this relationship. There is a reason, an important lesson to be learned. Are you ready to find out what it is?

Part II

Check Your Source

CHAPTER 3

I AM Connected

...

Over the years, Spirit has revealed to me that we all have similar lessons to learn. Key truths. Universal teachings. That said, depending on the specifics of your life—including factors like your family structure, culture, religion, traditions, environment, and your family's history of physical and mental health—some lessons will be harder for you to accept than others. Therein lies *your* work. We're going to go through the following seven lessons one by one because they're all transformative. As you make your way through each of them, be mindful of which ones stand out to you, either because they deeply resonate or because they trigger discomfort.

Resistance to a particular lesson is a clue that there's unfinished work for you to do in this area. Deep resonance is a clue that you're on to something important, even if you can't put your finger on it. For now, consider both of these feelings—resistance and resonance—as nudges to simply pay attention—the "why" will reveal itself in time. If a strong feeling doesn't arise in relation to a lesson, perhaps you've already done the necessary work. Neutrality is clear guidance that you've checked an assignment off your list. Still, I discourage skipping ahead because there is always something to be gleaned even from lessons you've already mastered. (To help you identify your top assignments, access the free assessment using the QR code at the back of the book.) Okay, let's get started.

Lesson 1: I AM Connected

I know I'm not breaking any new ground with this one. The idea that we're all connected and "all one" is a popular refrain. It's the through line in so many of our favorite songs, movies, and stories. But let me ask you this: What if it weren't just a nice idea but, instead, something you knew to be true? What would it be like to *feel* this truth?

Let me go ahead and answer this question for you. The knowing and *feeling* that you are connected to everyone on Earth by an energetic, unbreakable cord of invisible love and light that extends to the source of all energy has the potential to transform your life, because knowing and acting from this truth is one of life's biggest lessons.

In my readings with spirits who died a physical death without believing in the concept of an afterlife or a framework that connects all beings as one big family, related by energy, the importance of this lesson is validated over and over again. Where they were skeptical in life, spirits often jump up and down in readings, eager and excited to share the good news with their living loved ones: *I'm not alone . . . I'm surrounded by love . . . there is no isolation here . . . the feeling is one of inclusion, unity, acceptance, and connection.* They want their loved ones to feel the truth that they are now existing within.

What I have been shown is that we are all connected to the

highest vibrational energy of love and light that exists. Again, call it what you want—Source, Higher Power, Creator, God, the Universe, the Divine, All Love. We are connected to this energy because we were born from it, and we will return to it. It is our true home, where all our ancestral lines lead, forward and backward, past and future. In our present-day life, sparks of Spirit energy move through and dwell within us; to *feel* it is just a matter of tuning in to its frequency.

Admittedly, this is a big lesson to lead with, a lofty place to start. Even for me, it can sound esoteric, not tangible, or relatable enough, and I'm in the business of working in the clouds. Still, it's important to begin here because this lesson lays the foundation for all others. Over the years, what enlightened beings have communicated to me is that our relationship with Spirit is *the most important relationship of our lives*, and only once you strengthen it by reconnecting to it will you be able to successfully attend to more Earthly matters.

As someone who shares this lesson of connection with people every day, I've become very familiar with the counterargument, one that you may also be considering right now—*I was born alone, and I will die alone. Therefore, I am ultimately separate and alone.* Of course, it's true that we are each born into a tiny, individual human body. Even with the urging and loving push of our mothers and, for many of us, a doctor in the room helping to bring us out into the bright, new world, the experience of birth is solitary. We can make a similar case with death. No one else is truly sharing this individual experience with us. And yet, we each came into this world as a bundle of powerful spirit energy that connects us back home, to our true origins. In this respect, we are never alone. We may think we are, but on a deep soul level we know differently. We know that we are made up of love and light energy that never dies, but that only changes form, depending on where we are in the moment, in the material world or the spiritual world. Michael Newton explains it this way in *Journey of Souls*: "We exist in two worlds, the material and the spiritual . . . and it is our destiny to shuttle back and forth between these universes through space and time while we learn to master ourselves and acquire knowledge."

There's just one little wrinkle in this time-travel scenario, and that is: amnesia.

As soon as we're born into this physical world, we go blank. We forget the plan. We forget what we are and from where we came. And why, pray tell, would we forget something so important? It certainly begs the question, and the answer is, well, we can't handle the truth. Even on a soul level, it's *too much information*, and so we come into this life with a case of spiritual amnesia and this state of neutrality provides us with an unparalleled opportunity to wake up. To come back to our knowing. To remember who and what we are all over again: a spiritual being having a human experience. Remembering is the work.

If you're questioning the logic behind spending our lifetimes in an attempt to remember what we already know, spirits assure me that we choose to go blank when we return to Earth so that we can start anew. If we began our lives with memories from past lives or with an understanding of the bigger picture, not only would our tiny brains pop from TMI, but they would prevent us from experiencing the awe and wonder of childhood. Ignorance *is* bliss. Each of us deserves to experience the carefree play and magic of being a child, and to unravel our life lessons in a neutral state with a fresh set of eyes and an open mind and heart.

Furthermore, if we came into our bodies with a clear remembrance of the safe, warm, and fuzzy place we just left, we wouldn't be able to handle the extreme contrasts, polarities, and dualities of the Earth plane. Spirits share that we don't remember our true home because a certain amount of separation is necessary for us to have a full human experience that allows us to grow our souls in this lifetime.

I'll not soon forget the forthright young man who, with his grandfather, attended one of my large group seminars on soul contracts. When I invited questions from the audience, he raised his hand and asked in no-nonsense, teenage terms: "I don't get it. Why come here at all? Heaven sounds great, and Earth is hard."

I laughed and said, "You're right, but just like there comes a time when someone your age must leave the nest, the same holds true for our souls. If we stayed indefinitely in the safety and comfort of 'home,' we wouldn't be able to experience the hands-on learning that's possible on Earth with its inherent contrast and duality. It's fertile learning ground! Add to that, by finishing our homework in the same environment we started it (Earth), we can be much more efficient and productive at getting the job done. When we do finally return home, we get the chance to recharge, regroup, and be reminded of who and what we are before we dive back into the next round of our soul's curriculum, whether that be reincarnating again to learn more or continuing our work on the Other Side. We're all on a different track, but our lesson to learn is the same. As the saying goes, 'many paths, one truth.' We are not separate or alone. We are connected. We are one."

Mind Tricks

• • •

The work of remembering is no easy task. And what makes it so challenging is the limitation of our minds. Our souls know that we're connected to Spirit, but our minds don't share this sense of connection. While the mind is brilliant and has many admirable qualities, like staying on high alert to keep us safe, it can also go a bit off the rails in this pursuit to protect us from harm. It can easily slip into a frenetic, fearful state, not unlike a child who gets separated from their parents in a crowded airport and is suddenly lost and alone and *freaking out*. The mind is a master at tricking us into believing we are lost at the airport, even when we're no-where near an airport! We could be sitting in our favorite comfy chair at home and suddenly, out of nowhere, get hit with *oh shit* existential questions like "Who am I? Where am I?" that propel us into feelings of separation and disconnection from ourselves, each other, and from something *more*. So many of us manage to think our way into fearful states that we confuse with truth, and, as Dr. Nicole LePera writes in *How to Do the Work*, "our prac-ticed thoughts become our truth." And yet, the truth is that we are never separated from Spirit; we only *think* we are. That's the great illusion.

I've communicated with hundreds of spirits who express their regrets over how much of their lives they spent "in hell," down the rabbit hole of their minds, believing that they were alone. They wish they would have understood, or at least had some sense of, their connection to Spirit when they were still in a physical body because now that they are reconnected, they know and *feel* that there is no separation, only unity, and they urge their living loved ones to wake up to this truth *now*. As Don Miguel Ruiz writes in *The Four Agreements*, "When we start challenging our beliefs, you will find that most of the beliefs that guided you into the wounded mind are not even true. You will find that you suffered all those years of drama for nothing ... [because] the belief system that was put inside your mind is based on lies."

Mind Versus Soul

In order to survive in this world, we need executive functioning, deductive reasoning, and all the other smart functions of our minds. We also need the inspiration and quiet guidance that come from our souls. So then, the goal is not to rely on one over the other, but to encourage them to work in tandem. The mind and soul can perfectly complement each other when we allow them to do what they do best. When the soul is inspired, the mind will fearlessly lead.

Beliefs Have Energy

• • •

Remember, your physical body isn't the only part of you that's made up of energy. Beliefs, stories, and untruths have energy, too. The belief that we're disconnected and separate resides at a very low frequency; when we buy into this story, which so many of us tell ourselves, our energy lowers to match it. Over time, if we stay in alignment with this fearful belief, our energy can get stuck in this low place and affect our lives. "When unconscious storytelling becomes our default," Brené Brown writes in *Rising Strong*, "we often keep tripping over the same issue, staying down when we fall, and having different versions of the same problem in our relationships—we've got the story on repeat."

A story about disconnection on repeat can be unhealthy, even dangerous. For instance, during a group reading, I tapped into the spirit of a young man who overdosed on prescription drugs. Through a series of mental pictures that he flashed in my mind, I rewound to a news story I'd recently seen about the growing opioid epidemic alongside a bottle of pills. He then showed me the silhouette of himself as a young man dressed all in black, combined with fireworks exploding in the night sky, my "sign" that in life his energy was fragmented, fearful, ungrounded, and dark. I could *feel* him hiding from his fearful feelings; he was ashamed of them when, outwardly, he pretended to be fine. He clairvoyantly showed me a flash of Jim Carrey's character in *The Mask* to indicate that he wore a false face in public, which made him feel even more disconnected and alone in his private life. I then flashed on a dream visitation I'd had of my own father, sitting back in a recliner in a dimly lit study, with one leg crossed over the other, arms folded against his chest. I recognized what this meant: the crossed arms and legs indicated that he was "closed off" emotionally and mentally, unable to recognize his need for or to seek help, and the dimly lit study indicated a low-level "dim" energy in life. I understood that this young spirit had a similar life experience as my dad. He believed that he was alone, broken, and unfixable. I clairvoyantly saw this spirit in a cage, inhabiting the prison of the mind and stuck in the lower vibrations of fear.

And then, suddenly, a very different picture emerged.

The spirit of this young man showed me a rainbow and communicated that he was "wearing color" again, and no longer in a dark place. Where he'd felt energetically run-down on so many levels in life, he realized now that he didn't have to leave his body to free himself of his "living hell." Back in spirit form, he was reviewing his unfinished work, and at the top of the list was the understanding of interconnection and unconditional love and belonging. His cautionary message for his living loved ones was: what you *think* is what you *feel* is what you *become.* He showed me a white rose, which is my sign for forgiveness and purification, and communicated by flashing an image of his mother kneeling, suggesting that his family's willingness to pray for him, and forgive him, was helping him to heal. He was working hard in spirit to unlock his heart and raise his energy to a higher level of light and love for himself, and for those he left behind.

I want to take a moment here to acknowledge that I am not an expert on mental health issues, and in the brutal arena of suicide there are, of course, no simple answers. The guidance I continue to receive from my deceased father and my grandma Babe is that suicide is predominantly the result of and the manifestation of mental illness, and that it's essential we regard those who are suffering, or who suffered in this way, with compassion. Grandma Babe continues to remind me to share with others the importance of reframing the language around suicide, using the words *died by* rather than *committed.* If you or a loved one is struggling with thoughts of suicide, please reach out for professional help. For the

Suicide and Crisis Lifeline, dial 988 or dial the National Suicide Hotline at 800-273-8255.

Additional Insights on Suicide

To honor my own grandmother and father, who died by suicide, and to help those of you who also wrestle with what can feel like a bottomless well of unanswered questions left behind from a suicide, I offer the following insights that I've received from my spiritual guides.

Q: If we plan our lives and our "tests" before we're born, does that mean suicide is planned?

A: Suicide is never planned as an absolute, but it exists as a possibility or a high probability for some people. On an unconscious level, these souls bring in unhealed energy from a past life (unfinished homework), with the intention to heal, evolve, and pass their tests this time. If these souls again struggle along the way, the intention is that they ask for help and seek the necessary resources to guide them forward so that they bypass their potential for suicide and find the path that leads to healing and growth with the least amount of pain and struggle. Suicide will sometimes emerge as an optional exit point, if a soul feels like they cannot complete their work. I've channeled spirits who expressed that they became so burned out, run-down, and broken that they felt they could no longer "do life," a form of admission that they'd been overly ambitious in designing their blueprint. This is where mental illness can contribute to creating illusion and delusion. Spirits who died by suicide have shown me a torn map, to communicate that they had become separated from their relationship with Spirit and, as a result, felt lost in life.

Q: When do higher beings step in to prevent suicide?

A: If the individual (again on a "soul," and not on a "mind," level) has the slightest willingness or desire for help and healing, divine intervention occurs in the final moment before they're able to follow through on their act of suicide. To paraphrase my colleague Robert Schwartz, who says it succinctly: *every suicide that could have been prevented, was prevented.* If you've lost a loved one to suicide, embracing this truth can help alleviate guilt or self-blame for feeling that you could have stepped in to save a life. Nobody dies without their own consent, but the consent is at the *soul level* and not necessarily on a conscious human level. Spirits who died by suicide often relay to their still-living loved ones: No one failed me. No one was to blame. No one else was responsible. No one caused this. It was *my* choice. Please, let go of your guilt.

Q: Why would someone choose or plan to suffer and die this way?

A: When you embrace that our individual challenges and struggles are meant to teach and help us grow, then the greatest gift you can give a loved one who has died by suicide is to honor their choice, their plan for this lifetime. This doesn't mean you agree with or like it; it means only that you accept it as *their* choice and release *yourself* from their actions. Spirits of suicide come through with an urgency to encourage their living loved ones to live their own lives fully, to fulfill their own life's plan, and to release any responsibility for their choice. When we pray for or meditate on a spirit's highest truth and healing, we not only assist in elevating that spirit's soul, but also we help to heal ourselves.

Q: If suicide is the result of mental illness, are you saying that mental illness is predetermined?

A: Again, we know there is a genetic basis to many forms of mental illness, so in that sense, it is by design. But as well, life experience—including undergoing traumatic emotional or physical events that deeply impact our functioning—can lead to mental health problems, including depression and suicidal ideation.

For example, in a recent group reading two spirits came forward, acknowledging that they had impaired thinking in life as a result of certain events—one had a sepsis infection that caused acute brain dysfunction, and one had a degenerative brain disease (CTE, or chronic traumatic encephalopathy), the result of being a professional athlete who had sustained head injuries. While neither man had mental illness in his family, both developed a mental illness in life that ultimately led to their untimely demise.

Over the years, I've done many readings where spirits communicate that while they were never diagnosed with depression or another mental illness, they were extra sensitive to energy. They show me a sponge, my "sign" for an empath or a highly sensitive person. I've channeled spirits who communicate that their heightened sensitivity made them vulnerable to an energy imbalance, or what I refer to as "fragmented energy" or "shadow energy," which negatively influenced their thoughts, feelings, and behaviors in life. They urge their living loved ones to harness their energy and rise above the lower frequencies of fear and separation that create a Hell on Earth.

Change. Elevate. Grow.

• • •

If you find yourself resisting the idea of connection and dipping into separation, remember, this is your clue that your mind is running the show and potentially wreaking havoc with your energy. After many years of experimenting with a variety of techniques, from breath work to meditation, hypnosis, affirmations, and journaling, I've developed a three-step practice I recommend to my clients to help them reframe false stories about their lives and embrace and *feel* important lessons. It looks like this: **Change the narrative. Elevate your Energy. Grow the Feeling.** We will use this framework to help you engage with each of the seven lessons.

For example, let's start by changing the narrative that you are not connected:

I am all alone ⇨

I AM connected. I AM secure.

Once you change, or flip, the narrative, the next step is to elevate your energy by *imprinting* this lesson on your heart, and I recommend using affirmations to do this work, especially at times when you're feeling disconnected from yourself or the world around you:

I AM more than a body. I AM a spirit in a body, and I AM remembering who and what I AM. I AM love. I AM light. I AM one with the energetic vibration of Spirit. I AM interconnected to everyone, everywhere through Spirit energy. I AM THAT I AM.

Commit your affirmations to memory or jot them down on an index card or a sticky note that you affix to places you see throughout the day. Some clients write their affirmations down on pieces of paper that they stuff into their pockets, backpacks, and purses. Whatever way you choose, when said out loud or inwardly, inspiring and affirming words work to redirect and raise your energy, and when you specifically say "I AM THAT I AM," you are affirming that Spirit is where you are, that Spirit is within, and according to many mystics, when repeated, chanted, or reflected on, this specific mantra is believed to release deep *knowing* within you. José Luis Stevens, PhD, proposes in *How to Pray the Shaman's Way*, that *I* and *AM* are "two of the most powerful words we can ever utter. They are the formative words of Creation that align us with Spirit better than almost anything else we can say or do. Just thinking the phrase, I AM invokes the universal life force given to us by Spirit—that energy that keeps us alive moment by moment."

Big promises for such a simple phrase, but I've relied on it many times and I can attest to its power. On days when I'm feeling disconnected or generally "off," I'll take a moment and meditate on "I AM THAT I AM" to reactivate my knowing that I'm an extension of Spirit. And, really, I can feel a lightening of my energy, as if a swirling light wave has reconnected to and recharged my internal battery.

Elevate with Your True Colors

• • •

While reframing a story, a script, or a belief as a positive statement, mantra, or invocation is a powerful practice, it doesn't always go far enough on its own. Beyond the daily practice of verbal repetition, I recommend that you also work on elevating your energy to align with the **color** of this new belief.

Let me explain—

In addition to thinking of beliefs and the feelings associated with those beliefs as currents of energy, you can also envision them as colors, on a scale from the brightest light to the darkest shadows. For instance, the belief that I am alone and separate vibrates at the same short energetic wavelength as the color red, at 432 THz, whereas the feeling that I am connected and one with Spirit vibrates at a faster light frequency of 700 to 789 THz, the color range between deep purple and violet. I know it sounds pretty far-out, but there is a scientific basis for this idea. We know that light is energy, and the specific wavelength, frequency, and quantity of light energy determines its color. While the human eye can perceive light only in the frequency range of, plus or minus, 400 to 700 THz, we can *feel* color vibrations on a wider spectrum that affects our physical body as well as our thoughts and emotions. In other words, we innately react both physiologically and psychologically to colors as energetic frequencies that affect our internal frequency.

Drawing parallels between color and our physical health is widely accepted in popular medicine, and the correlation between feelings and wavelengths is deeply integrated in holistic health, and specifically within the chakra system. A predominant principle of the practice is that each chakra in the body corresponds to a vibration of light, of color. Anodea Judith, author of *Chakras* and founder of Sacred Centers, a teaching organization, likens chakras to precious radiant jewels of energy, spinning in colorful splendor, strung together like beads on a necklace. "If you think of the primordial energy of the cosmos streaming down into you," Judith writes in *Chakras*, "then your body is like a prism that breaks that energy down into different colors or frequencies." These whirling centers of life-force energy run up and down your energetic body at various speeds, and the seventh chakra, which is located in the crown of your head and broadly associated with awakening, cosmic awareness, and enlightenment, vibrates at a light wave frequency that matches the color of violet. Author and speaker Caroline Myss, who has explored the fields of human consciousness, spirituality and mysticism, health, energy medicine, and the science of medical intuition has written extensively on chakras and the energetic body. She sees a correlation between the seventh chakra and its effects on our feelings and our belief system, as do I. When this energy system is clean, spinning, and emanating a purple-ish or golden hue, we feel connected to Spirit, to that something bigger than ourselves. Conversely, when your crown energy is cloudy, clogged, and spinning off-balance, you're likely to feel off-balance—fearful, separate, disconnected and alone, stuck in your head and thinking too much.

In readings, spirits and higher enlightened beings often appear to me as colors, and over the years, I've learned that the color they identify as is a vibrational match to their "grade level" or degree of evolution on the Other Side. I'm no longer surprised to discover that a spirit that appears to me as purple, indigo blue, magenta, or violet are the most highly advanced and evolved, sometimes hovering at the angelic level. And remember the Council of Elders I referred to earlier, the group of master teachers and enlightened beings that greet spirits once they've crossed over and begun the process of reviewing their life? These beings often appear to me in readings wearing purple robes or as an apparition of violet and overlapping golden light. I realized after a recent rereading of *Destiny of Souls* that what I've clairvoyantly "seen" for years lines up again with Michael Newton's findings, specifically his ranking of the spiritual evolution of a soul based on its primary core colors.

Where I clairvoyantly see the color and clairsentiently feel the vibration of spirits, a lot of healers tap into the energy of chakras and auras when working with human clients on physical, mental, emotional, and spiritual levels. For the past four years, I've worked with Jakki Smith Leonardini, who studied with internationally renowned spiritual teacher and author Denise Linn. She cultivated her skill as a clairvoyant and energy healer under the tutelage of Michael Bates, with whom she trained for several years in techniques developed at the Berkeley Psychic Institute. Jakki is the first of her kind to teach me how to manage and harness my energy with the use of color. She refers to the process as "running energy" and uses the visualization of different colors funneling through the body to help recalibrate our energetic system. "We are electromagnetic beings living in an electromagnetic universe. Our vibration is unique to us and composed of light and shadow frequencies of energy, and our feelings are frequencies of energy that are magnified in color and tone," explains Jakki.

Every week working with Jakki is different, based on what I need in the moment, and the visualization I'll lead you through in a moment is a collaboration of Jakki's and my process of chakra healing and reconnecting with Spirit energy and with the truth that we are not alone.

Pick a Color

• • •

When I started playing around with the idea of adding color as a method for shifting our beliefs, I received validation that I was on the right track. As it was, I was organizing my notes for this section of the book on President's Day. My youngest, Haven, was home from school, and after failing to hold the attention of her older siblings, she asked me to "pleasssseeeee" play with her. After several pouty trips in and out of my home office, I finally surrendered to my then five-(going on fifteen!)-year-old and said, "Okay, let's take a walk outside."

Hand in hand, we walked to the nearby shopping district, and as we approached our local toy store, she pulled my hand. "Let's go in!"

I followed her into the store as she made a beeline to a bin of rings. She pulled one out and turned to me with wide eyes. "Mommy, it's so pretty. Can I get it?" On closer look, I realized that Haven was holding a mood ring, you know, the ones with the stones that supposedly change colors according to your mood, like black for stressed and pink for happy. Before I could answer her request for the ring, Haven abandoned the bin and was on to the next toy, a Color Ball where you match up colors like a Rubik's Cube. "Mommy, look. Can I get it?" It took me a minute to put it together that Spirit was using Haven as a messenger to validate the color aspect of the book. And because signs often come in threes, I wasn't entirely surprised when on our walk home a car passed with the following license plate: 777 RRH, my exact initials in combination with a number sequence that is translated in my field as a "sign" to mean: *Congratulations! You've listened well to your Divine Guidance. Trust that you're on the right path and keep going.* With the validation I needed, and with Haven temporarily entertained, I returned to my home office to write this section on color, feeling Spirit guiding me along. And then, as if to underscore the guidance, later that evening Haven asked to watch the movie *Inside Out*. It didn't hit me until we started watching it together that in the story, emotions are personified as colors! Yellow for joy and blue for sadness. I had to laugh. Again, Haven was stepping in to act as my messenger from Spirit. Message received!

Exercise

. . . .

Wash Yourself with Gold

In addition to repeating the I AM mantra to align with the truth that you are not separate but connected to something much bigger and brighter than how you may feel in the moment, you will "run the color of gold" throughout your body to push out fear, illusion, and confusion and raise your energy to align with Spirit. I've specifically chosen gold for this exercise because gold is often interpreted as the color of love and truth in its purest form. When I work with Jakki, she invites "divine golden truth" to run through my crown chakra to connect me directly to Spirit, and you will do the same.

To begin: Get present. Our point of power for shifting beliefs and redirecting our energy is when we are fully feeling and aware of our body and our surrounding environment in real time. When we become caught up in rerun thoughts of the past or jumping forward into the future, our energy becomes fragmented and dips into a lower frequency, which widens the gap between us and Spirit. Past- and future-tripping where we dwell in the past and imagine an unpredictable future creates a feeling of being disconnected.

Next, close your eyes. Take several deep breaths and sit up straight with your feet on the ground and your hands resting in your lap. Pull your shoulder blades back and drop them down, and feel your chest push out and forward. Now imagine Spirit as a magnificent and massive golden sun of heart-swelling love and light, burning and vibrating with powerful and radiant intensity. (If visualization is a challenge for you, use your physical eyes. As a visual prompt, sometimes I will hold one of my favorite gold jewelry pieces in my hands and imagine breathing in the energy of golden light as I focus my attention and intention on it.)

Once you have a mental picture or a visual representation of Spirit secure in your mind, descend a cord of bright, golden light through the crown of your head and down into your heart, locking it into place. This cord, or pipeline of golden energy, carries within it the essence of the I AM energy. It radiates the truth of you, the light that you are. Next, with your hand over your heart, say:

"I AM here, willing and ready to receive an upgrade to my energy. I invite the golden light and healing love of the I AM presence that exists within me, around me, and that is me. I allow this light to flood and fill me on all levels and layers of my being now. Restore me back to the knowing that I AM a brilliant light. I AM connected, in all directions of time and space, in all ways, today, tomorrow, and always through the energy of radiant golden light."

Change It + Run It + Tap It

• • •

As we unpack each lesson throughout the book, I will provide you with some of my favorite tools that I use to work through my own assignments, and how they may also help to propel you forward.

"Tapping" is one that I discovered in 2000 when I was enrolled in a holistic healing school in Farmington, Michigan. I've found it to be a very useful tool over the years, and if you're not yet familiar with it, I'm excited to share it with you now. Tapping, more formally known as the emotional freedom technique (EFT), is based on the combined principles of ancient Chinese acupressure and modern psychology and is an effective tool to shift your energy by releasing emotional toxins and false beliefs from your system. I've practiced tapping to break free from unhealthy cycles and patterns, chronic physical pain, and compulsions. It has also helped me to reduce stress and anxiety, and let go of grief, guilt, and regrets. I combine "changing the narrative" + "running energy" + "tapping" to fully integrate the lessons into my mind, body, and spirit and shift my vibration up the energetic scale. Here's how it works:

As you run your energy with the color of gold, you will also tap on the following meridian points, areas of the body through which energy flows. Akin to the Chinese medicine practice of acupuncture and acupressure, by tapping on these meridian points, you release stuck and stagnant energy that can create both physical and emotional imbalance and restore it to a healthier flow state.

A few things to keep in mind when tapping: use firm but gentle pressure, like you're tapping on a desk; tap with four fingers or the first two, index and middle; tap on either side of the body or a combination of both, as the meridian points are symmetrical.

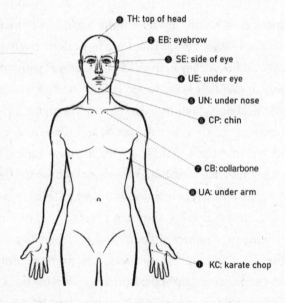

TH: top of head
EB: eyebrow
SE: side of eye
UE: under eye
UN: under nose
CP: chin
CB: collarbone
UA: under arm
KC: karate chop

Karate Chop Point: This is the outer edge of the hand, between the pinky and wrist. This is the starting point, where we tap with our fingers on one hand, on the side of the other hand, while you focus on and repeat your set up statement three times in a row, out loud, noticing how you feel as you do.

Eyebrow Point (EB): The space in-between where the eyebrows begin, closest to the bridge of the nose.

Side of Eye (SE): On the temple bone directly along the outside of either eye.

Under Eye (UE): On the bone directly under either eye.

Under Nose (UN): The area directly beneath the nose and above the upper lip.

Chin Point (CP): This is the area just below your bottom lip and above the chin, right in the crease.

Collarbone Point (CB): Starting from where your collarbones meet in the center, go down an inch and out an inch on either side.

Under Arm (UA): On your side, about four inches beneath the armpit.

Top of Head (TH): Directly on the crown of your head.

As you tap on the first "karate chop" point (illustrated on the diagram), repeat the following set up statements three times. Choose the sentiments that most resonate with you or feel free to make up your own, either repeating the same or different statements each time.

- Even though I feel so deeply sad/disconnected/alone . . . I AM connected to loving, healing Spirit energy that exists within me, around me, and that is me.
- Even though I feel isolated/lonely/unsafe . . . I AM connected, through space and time, today, tomorrow, and always through the energy of gold.
- Even though I feel scattered/lost/afraid . . . I AM connected, and I accept myself and how I feel.

After tapping on the "karate chop point," you will follow with a round or two of *feeling* statements that affirm the truth of how you feel. Keep it simple. As you tap on the remaining eight meridian points illustrated in the diagram on page 78—starting at the eyebrow point and ending at the top of the head—express an emotion that's got you down. It could be a single word ... "isolated," "lonely," "scared" ... or even a single sound ... "ugh," "yuck."

After you finish your rounds of tapping on all eight meridian points, do the full sequence again—starting at the eyebrow point and ending at the top of the head—while repeating the following I AM statements again (or feel free to create your own):

- I AM connected to loving, healing Spirit energy that exists within me, around me, and that is me.
- I AM connected, through space and time, today, tomorrow, and always through the energy of gold.
- I AM connected, and I accept myself and how I feel.

Bonus Material! To access a complimentary video of this tapping exercise, use the QR code at the back of the book.

The act of tapping "out" low-frequency feelings and tapping "in" higher energy sends a calming signal to our amygdala, the part of the brain responsible for triggering the stress response in our bodies. Tapping on these meridian points sends a memo to your mind that it's safe to relax, that there's no real threat or danger. When the body is back in parasympathetic, or relaxation, mode, the immune system, digestive system, reproductive system, and endocrine system can also relax and return to optimal functionality. Probably the most remarkable study regarding tapping and stress hormones was conducted by Dr. Dawson Church and published in the *Journal of Nervous and Mental Disease*. The 2012 study found that EFT tapping lowered levels of the stress hormone cortisol more significantly than traditional talk therapy or resting, and parallel research indicates tapping may be an effective treatment for anxiety, depression, and PTSD.

Grow the Feeling through Inspired Action

• • •

The energetic vibration of Spirit *feels* like unity and security, and through utilizing visualizations and practices like tapping, you may start to naturally feel more connected and secure. Add to that, the best way I know to grow and *embody* a new feeling, one that brings us closer to heaven, is to actively participate in activities that inspire connection, unity, and security.

On a recent big audience Zoom reading, I was able to demonstrate how this practice might help a young woman who was stuck in her own version of the conditioned belief: *I am alone and separate*. A few hours before the call, I found a gold coin in the middle of my closet floor, and since it appeared to have dropped out of the sky, I closed my eyes and asked my guides if they had anything to do with my finding it. I clairvoyantly saw the coin paired with jewelry, specifically a necklace, and that it was intended as a sign for a woman I'd be reading in my group later that day. And sure enough, when I started the reading several hours later, I again "saw" the coin alongside a spirit, a father figure. I put two and two together and said to the group, "Is anyone wearing a coin around their neck who lost a father?"

A woman in the virtual audience tentatively raised her hand. I read her screen name, Sarah, and then accessed her microphone. "Hi, Sarah, are you wearing a coin necklace? I'm here with a male spirit, a father figure, who is showing me a coin."

She went wide-eyed and pulled out a chain from underneath her sweater. She leaned forward and said, "I don't know if you can see this. It's an angel coin that my father gave to me before he died." She then started to cry, which triggered many tears in the audience.

Even though we were communicating over a computer screen, I could clairsentiently feel Sarah's heaviness as my own, like I was wearing a weighted blanket. This is one of my "signs" that a person is depressed, even if they are presenting themselves differently. I asked cautiously, "Have you been feeling low?"

She broke. "Yes, I feel so isolated and alone. I feel like I've been teetering in the eleventh hour."

"Your father in spirit is with you," I said, hoping to comfort her. "And he's smiling. He says that in life he didn't believe in God or in an afterlife of any kind and he wants you to know that he was wrong. He's showing me two puzzle pieces, as if he's put it together. He remembers now that we are all connected, not alone."

Sarah nodded her head and said, "He was a skeptic for sure. Probably where I got it from."

"Well, now he is saying otherwise, and he wants you to *remember* this truth, too. He's flashing a piano in my mind's eye now. Does this make sense to you? Did he play the piano?"

"I play," Sarah clarified. "Although I haven't in a while. Dad always encouraged me to play."

"He wants you to start playing again. He's showing me that this activity is how you elevate your energy. It gets you out of your low place and helps you to connect to your dad." I explained to the group that music vibrates at a high frequency, and either by listening to it, creating it with instruments, our own voices, or even by ringing a simple bell, sound can break up dense and stagnant energy within us, releasing and elevating our energy to a higher frequency. Music does actually lift our spirits because it is aligned with the frequency of the spirit world. This is why the deceased often communicate with their living loved ones through music. I addressed the entire Zoom group, "If a song comes on the radio or randomly pops up in a music stream that reminds you of a passed loved one at the exact time you are thinking about them, it is likely not a coincidence. If a piece of music or a song lyric pops into your head that offers you a message that resonates with you, this probably is not just a chance circumstance. More than likely, a departed loved one is orchestrating the whole thing to let you know that they are with you."

Sarah jumped in. "Oh my gosh, the other day a piano piece randomly started playing on Spotify and it made me think about Dad. I didn't recognize the artist, so I made a point to check the title."

"And?" I asked in eager anticipation.

"The artist is a man named Alexis Ffrench and . . ."—she paused—"you're not going to believe this, but the name of his album is *Truth*. I remember because I liked it so much, I wrote it down."

"That's exactly how it works." I practically jumped through my screen. "Your dad wants you to know the *truth*. His message to you is that you're not alone and when you feel isolated or depressed or cut off from the world or from the presence of your dad, that is the moment when you sit down and play your piano because it immediately raises your energy out of a depressed state. It lifts and transports you to higher ground. For you, this is the action that will help you reconnect with yourself and *feel* connected to something bigger. And as you begin to shift your feelings of separateness, you help to heal a generational struggle."

For Sarah, playing the piano is a form of inspired action. What is it for you? It might be meditating, walking in nature, or singing in a choir. I gravitate toward a combination of nature and music. I specifically enjoy listening to the solfeggio frequencies. Have you heard of these? They refer to specific tones of sound that date back to ancient history, chanted by Gregorian monks and in ancient Indian Sanskrit chants. The work of physician and researcher Dr. Joseph Puleo proposes that the solfeggio frequencies can profoundly affect the conscious and subconscious mind and bring the energetic body back into balance. According to his mathematical numeral reduction, there are six solfeggio frequencies, and the highest, clocking in at an impressive 963 hertz and referred to as the "frequency of the Gods," is believed to inspire a sense of oneness and unity. When I'm feeling disconnected, alone, or insecure I like to pop in my earbuds and tune in to this frequency as I take a meditative walk outside. For me, they work every time. (Find hundreds of free solfeggio frequencies available for download online.)

CHAPTER 4

I AM Remembering

...

Almost as soon as Elizabeth sat down in my small-group reading, I could feel the presence of her husband coming through as butterflies in my stomach, my physical sign that a spirit is eager and excited to communicate with the living. These feelings were accompanied by a clairvoyant image of my husband. I asked Elizabeth, "Do you know why your husband would be flashing in my mind an image of my own husband, Chris?"

"His name was Chris, too," she validated.

A complete parallel.

"He's flashing me a mental picture of the heart and I'm getting the sense that he died suddenly and quickly, and with no pain." I put the signs together and asked, "Was it a heart attack?"

Elizabeth started to cry. "He was only fifty-five years old, and by the time I got upstairs and found him, it was too late. I gave him CPR, but I couldn't save him," she nearly whispered.

"He's saying that it was his time to go. It was all part of his plan and you were never meant to save his life." As I said this, I "saw" a nurse's cap, my sign for the caregiver archetype. I wondered aloud if Elizabeth was a literal nurse in her day-to-day life, and she confirmed, "Yes, which makes it all the more awful. I should have been able to help him and"—she dissolved into tears again—"I feel like I failed him."

I explained to Elizabeth what I've been guided to pass on from the spirit world to the living. "If it wasn't supposed to be his 'exit point,' a form of divine intervention would have occurred to stop it from happening. And he's clearly communicating that it was his time to go."

When a spirit taps their finger on the face of a watch, combined with a flash of an open book, their Book of Life, I understand it to mean that their death happened at the *right time* according to their soul contract, and this is what Chris's spirit was showing me now.

I continued, "He's placing his palms together and thanking you for always showing up, for offering your love and care, not only to him but also to so many others in your life. You have fulfilled that role, and now your lesson is to trust that there is a plan at work, and to forgive yourself for something you could not have controlled. His death is not yours to own."

Elizabeth dropped her head into her hands. Finally, she lifted her eyes to meet mine and said, "I've been haunted by this for two years. I play it over and over in mind, thinking it was somehow my fault for failing to save the most important person in my life."

"He's shaking his head no, it was not your fault and now it's time for you to embrace life again. Why is he showing me an image of a husky dog?"

"That's my dog, Rascal." She lightened.

"Rascal is your furry Earth angel, here to help you through a rough time and to teach you to keep your heart open through this period of grief."

I explained to Elizabeth that pets often step in to provide us with unconditional love during times in our life when we need extra support.

"Your husband, Chris, is now imprinting the letter *M* in my mind with a bouquet of roses, my sign for romantic love. Does that make sense?"

She took in a sharp breath. "I've been casually dating his friend Mark, but I'm not sure if it's heading anywhere."

"Chris is waving his hand forward, giving his permission to pursue it. Mark will help you heal and move forward. And finally," I said, "Chris is showing me a heart-shaped rock. When you come across one, know that this is his sign to you, to remind you to be strong like a rock, and to keep your heart open. And even though he is not here in person, he is with you forever."

Elizabeth's mouth dropped open as she dug her hand into her pocket and pulled out a, *you guessed it*, heart-shaped rock.

"I found it this morning when I was out walking. That is crazy."

"Wow. That *is* crazy," I agreed. "Keep it in your pocket as a reminder that your life is unfolding according to plan and to trust that all is well, even within the struggle."

A Plan at Work

· · ·

Every day I meet with clients like Elizabeth who, in addition to their deep desire to connect to their deceased loved ones, seek clarity around the events in their lives. They want to know the "why" behind the breakup, the layoff, the unexpected medical diagnosis, the addiction, the loved one who died. In the face of their confusion, I pass on what I've learned from Spirit: we each come into this world with lessons we must learn in order to grow in this lifetime and spiritually evolve in the next. Our individual challenges were put into play *before* we were born, and it's up to each of us to unravel the meaning at the heart of them. Though at times our lives may feel extremely challenging, our spirit knows what our mind forgets.

This is Lesson 2: I AM remembering.

There is a rhyme and a reason to the messiness and the struggle. There is a plan to how my life is unfolding, and within it are lessons that are part of my assignment to master.

This lesson can be a hard one to digest. On an unconscious level, you know what you signed up for, but on a conscious level your mind has forgotten the plan. And without a clear vision, a sense of the bigger picture, it's human nature to slip into distrust, particularly when you're trying to make sense of hard things.

On what should have been a beautiful spring day in 2000, Julie and Doug lost their six-year-old daughter, Lauren, when she was hit and killed by their neighborhood school bus driver at the bottom of their driveway. A truly inconceivable, tragic event. When I first met Julie and Doug nearly seventeen years ago, they were in deep grief. On the day we sat down together for the reading, I prayed for connection and protection and invited in messages from beyond that would help and heal them both. Right away, Lauren's spunky spirit came barreling through with a strong message for her parents: I'm here and I'm okay.

With that healing knowledge, Julie and Doug began to grow through their grief and, in 2008, when Julie felt called to begin an organization called GrieveWell that would provide help to people struggling in the early stages of their grief, she suspected Lauren's death was part of a bigger plan. In subsequent readings over the next few years, I was able to reassure Julie that, indeed, the painful experience of Lauren's death was by design and had resulted in her and Doug being afforded the opportunity to help others.

During a reading in March of 2020, fully twenty years after Lauren's death, Julie brought up the subject of her ongoing work toward forgiveness of the bus driver. I suggested that she continue to ask for guidance to see Lauren's death through a wider lens, "beyond what your human eyes have been able to see."

Spirits share that forgiveness is what ultimately releases the living and the dead. Forgiveness is the door through which miracles enter, and in the case of Julie and Doug, it did eventually open, and a miracle slipped through. Later that year, I received an email from Julie that was raw and vulnerable and that she graciously agreed to let me include in these pages. In it, she shared how she and Doug had been working hard to put their trust in a bigger plan. She wrote:

> We walked in the darkness of grief for so long, felt every emotion that comes with a sudden, violent, preventable loss at the hands of someone whom we trusted. We still struggle with

forgiveness. I can so easily remember my white-hot anger at the people from the school who should have been managing this young lady and who should have never put her behind the wheel of a school bus, a vehicle which symbolizes our kids' independence and an early and safe separation from their parents. My human mind is still so angry, but when I connect to my "higher self" and my heart through meditation, I can get to a place of knowing that the bus driver was simply playing a role in our story, like an actor in a play. Still, I float in between the space of accepting that Lauren was going to leave this plane earlier than I wanted or expected and hanging on to my rage toward the people and circumstances surrounding her death. I wish I could release blame and fully forgive, but I think the point of being human is working toward forgiveness as a life-long pursuit, like exercise and following a healthy diet. It's a practice you must return to regularly, all week, all year, every day of your life. I think when someone is significantly harmed or hurt by another, the forgiveness practice can last a lifetime. I know that losing Lauren has forced me to work on forgiving, and maybe this is a hidden blessing in her death.

The clear blessing in all of this is that our readings with you over the years changed the trajectory of our grief and it turned Doug from a total skeptic to total believer. Once you told us that death is not the end and the spirit lives on, we started a practice of talking to Lauren every day, inviting her spirit to family gatherings. And just like you said it would happen, we've seen so many signs over the years that she is still with us! You told us to look for ladybugs, butterflies and bees and they appear at random times and places just as you predicted. It is absolutely amazing when she shows us signs, and even more delightful is to realize that she is still our sweetheart Lauren, now in spirit, and filled with wonder of the world!

Add to that, our organization has grown WAY bigger than I dreamed it could have. What I often say about grief is: when you can name it, you can tame it. Our webinars help give people the words to explain their indescribable yearning and sadness, and now I finally see that THIS is what Lauren was hinting at . . . a bigger purpose for us all.

As a Divine synchronicity, in a follow-up reading with Julie while I was writing this chapter—twenty-two years after Lauren's death—her spunky spirit came through again, and this time she flashed an image of my own daughter's nightshirt in my mind's eye, black and red cheetah print to be exact. When I asked Julie why I might be seeing this specific pattern, she gasped and recalled the memory of giving her daughter Lauren a new set of pajamas the night before she died with the same cheetah print. Julie said she hadn't thought about this memory in two decades and wondered why Lauren would bring it up now.

"She's picking up right where you left off," I said confidantly.

Even though twenty-two years had passed, time is just an illusion in the spirit world, and Lauren was recalling the memory as if it were yesterday.

"She's using this memory to remind you that you did your best to take care of her right up until the end, and she's urging you to allow yourself to *feel* that swell of love and tenderness for her just before you lost her, before the heartbreak, the anger, the pain."

Julie felt overcome with emotion at the recollection of this memory but said it would help her to continue to open her heart toward forgiveness and acceptance. Later that evening, when I asked Haven to get changed for bed, she chose the cheetah nightshirt. Of course she did! Lauren's cheeky spirit was at play with my own daughter, orchestrating another sign to validate her eternal presence more than two decades after her physical death.

Making Sense of Tragedy

* * *

I have worked with many parents who have lost children—in pregnancy, infanthood, childhood, and early adulthood—and in my opinion, this is the greatest loss one can experience, and my thoughts, prayers, love, and light go out to those who have lost children. And yet again, what Spirit has shown me is a "line out the door" of selfless souls who *choose* to incarnate to help the people around them learn something very specific, like the importance of letting go and forgiving, or to assist them in finding their faith and connection to Spirit, and once their assignment is complete, they return back "home." For grieving individuals and families who have lost a child and are feeling pain, please know that your child is not in pain. Their soul lives on. What I've come to understand is that these "volunteers" have been here before—many times, even—and have already passed their own life lessons, and because of this they can afford to sacrifice *this life* for the express purpose of serving others. From a human perspective it might seem unthinkable that anyone would assist in what may seem like a needless tragedy, but these advanced souls regard it as a privilege to act in service to others. The advanced soul who signs up to exit this world suddenly, tragically, or at a young age knows ahead of time that their death will serve as an opportunity for their surviving loved ones to learn and evolve.

Assuming you can wrap your mind around what I've just put before you, how then, do I account for the traumatic events like natural disasters, a pandemic, or a war that leads to countless deaths? As senseless, random, or chaotic as these types of events appear to be, seen through a spiritual lens, they are still part of a bigger plan. On an unconscious level, no spirit leaves the body without its consent. So whether it's a natural disaster or a mass shooting, it is very likely that the victims agreed to a "group exit point." That is, prior to coming into this life, they made an agreement to come together at an exact place and time to volunteer their lives as a means to unite a community, and also inspire individual lessons in forgiveness. Understand that every death has the potential to create a profound transformation for the living, given that those left behind choose to learn from the experience and allow it to shift their own energy up toward the higher vibration of love. I call these *shake up to wake up* moments.

My line of work becomes particularly sensitive when violent acts become headline news. I'm frequently flooded with emails from people all over the world who reach out and ask: *Why did this happen? What does it mean? If there is a God, why would he/she/they/it allow this evil act to take place? And what of the individuals who commit these horrible acts?* Again, some events are impossible to justify and so difficult to understand, and personally, I struggle with making sense of the senseless. While it doesn't make it any less awful and hard to bear witness to, what Spirit has revealed to me is that some people will agree to play a dark role in life to awaken and enlighten humanity, creating a collective energetic shift up. An example of this is a soldier who kills civilians in a war. A war may create a global swell of generosity, compassion, and support for true boots on the ground that results in a political shift in power. In other words, it is not for nothing. In other cases, a soul will intentionally choose a darker role in life to further their own growth and evolution—truly, the hardest way to learn.

In other instances, however, like the young man who shot dead nineteen young children and two adults at an elementary school in Uvalde, Texas, in 2022, an individual has abused the power of their own free will to carry out horrendous acts on innocent people. People ask me, *Rebecca, do you believe in evil?* The answer is: yes. I believe we are all capable of darkness, just as we are all capable of absolute light and love. We each have free will. How we choose to show up in the world is our birthright. What I've come to understand through my mediumship work is that people who commit evil acts have slipped out of alignment from Spirit and their own light, and they're choosing, if even unconsciously, from the frequency of shadow, which is rooted in fear, illusions, and delusions.

Do negative human acts of free will supersede a spirit's prewritten life plan? Sometimes yes, sometimes no. We each set up pre-birth plans, which include a loose script of the lessons we need to learn and to teach in relationship with others. That said, what we do with our script is not set in stone. The details of how our life plays out is subject to change due to our free will—our choices—in any given moment.

All of us, myself included, can dip into shadow and operate from our false beliefs, childhood wounds, traumas, and fears. The frightened parts of our personality are there. Our "work" isn't to eliminate our darkness so much as it is our responsibility to become conscious and aware of it and then, be intentional about our choices. Get in a habit of asking yourself: From what frequency am I making this choice? Is this coming from a light or shadow frequency? Another way to ask this is: What would love do? What choice would love make? When we are in energetic alignment with love and light, it is easier and joyful, even, to make choices that uplift us and elevate the people and the world around us.

The Bigger Picture

• • •

I meet people every day who have turned away from connection to a unifying source because they're suffering. When we lose someone dear to us or lose an important piece of our lives—be it a job, a slip in our financial security, or a threat to our health or safety—it's instinct to question whether there is any divine order to our lives. In instances like these, Spirit shares that we can choose either to move in the direction of losing our trust, or pivot in the opposite direction. Diving deeper into trust when our world is on fire can feel counterintuitive, but within your struggle is *your greatest opportunity for healing and growth.* Over the years, spirits have shared that they struggled to understand the bigger purpose to their lives while they were alive, making it nearly impossible for them to appreciate the teaching moments, or growth opportunities. Earth can be a tough place to live, and human beings are susceptible to feelings of separation, segregation, fragmentation, competition, scarcity, limitation, illusion, delusion, desperation, and distrust—all of which are low-level frequencies. When these dense energies are present in our bodies, it can be challenging, at best, to see any experience from a higher perspective. And when we operate from a belief system that asserts "bad things happen to me," our energy can get stuck in a low-down place. Albert Einstein taught that "everything is energy and that's all there is to it. Match the frequency of the reality you want, and you cannot help but get that reality. It can be no other way. This is not philosophy. This is physics." To take it a step further, our thoughts and feelings hold a vibration that can evolve into matter. When we vibrate at the low vibration of victimization, cynicism, and powerlessness, our life experience, our day-to-day reality, will lower to match it.

Voices from Beyond

• • •

I met with a man named Daniel who was seeking answers and guidance around his career goals. He didn't understand why things weren't happening as he expected. He explained that he'd been struggling to launch a big project for the past six years, and now he had created a self-imposed deadline for the end of the month, and he sought my help in reaching it. His spirit guides lovingly but directly called him out for failing to do his homework. He had disconnected from Spirit by abandoning his daily practice of prayer and meditation and had been operating solely from his fearful mind, which put him in a constant state of "efforting," trying to control outcomes and make things happen, rather than allowing them to happen. All of this work, which wasn't bearing desirable fruit, was dropping him deeper into a pool of stuck and stagnant energy. I clairvoyantly saw Daniel as a hamster running on a wheel, going nowhere with great frustration and fatigue. While he was willing, he said, to continue to pursue his goal, he continued to make excuses for why things weren't working out and blamed bad luck. His attitude that "life sucks" along with habitual thoughts like *bad things happen to me* had him stuck in the lowest vibrational frequency—victim consciousness.

When he asked me what he ought to do to shift his luck, the spirit of Daniel's paternal grandfather came forward, sharing that he was acting as Daniel's guide for this particular life assignment, and that by doing so he would help to redeem a family legacy of victimization mentality that was passed down at least three generations. Daniel's grandfather impressed upon me that his own son, Daniel's father, had also failed this lesson in life and was working on the Other Side to learn accountability. Hearing this, Daniel acknowledged that his dad had worked hard in life but was unsuccessful.

"I watched him struggle to make ends meet," he said.

"Your grandfather is saying 'work smarter, not harder.' You have internalized the false belief that you have to work tirelessly to make money, and you are unconsciously repeating a family pattern that you learned in childhood and witnessed throughout your lifetime of trying to control outcomes and then blaming others when things don't work out the way you'd hoped." I said, "You must break this energetic agreement with believing you are a victim in your own life. Your grandfather is showing me that this way of thinking over time has created a self-fulfilling prophecy. You believe that things will go wrong, and they do." As I said this to Daniel, I was clairvoyantly shown a framed picture of Paramahansa Yogananda on Daniel's desk, who I recognized as the Indian Hindu monk, yogi, and famous guru. I asked him about it, and Daniel gasped. "I have a photograph of him on my desk right *now*. He's always inspired me."

"His energy is coming through"—I smiled—"to validate that you are not alone and to trust in and have faith in your path. If you can surrender some of your fear that puts you in a state of controlling, the next steps will be revealed to you." And on that note, I heard the name "Frank"—very loud and very clear. I asked Daniel, "Who is Frank, alive, not dead?"

Daniel looked at me in shock. "That's my grandfather's name! And also, there is a Frank who's a very influential person in my line of work. I've been planning for weeks to reach out to him and set up a meeting."

"Your guides are saying that this Frank is an important piece of the puzzle, a next step to take."

"Do they say anything else?" Daniel wanted to know.

"They won't reveal how it all plays out, A to Z, because your part can heavily influence the outcome. This is why it's so important to get out of your head and into your heart. Break agreements with your family's way of victim thinking and embrace trust and faith. That's my best advice."

Six weeks later, Daniel emailed me with an update. He relayed that he was working with Frank to reroute a better way to launch his project. I congratulated him and also reminded him that while Frank was an important piece of the puzzle, Spirit was his ultimate source, not any individual person. "As you move forward, remember Spirit's message: surrender control and trust in the path unseen. You're well on your way!"

The Illusion of Control

• • •

If your life feels like one hard knock after another, consider how much you're trying to control situations rather than allowing events in your life to unfold. When we overthink, over-do, and over-effort the big and small details of our lives, we create resistance that takes us out of the natural flow of our energy. The difference between putting forth our best effort and over-efforting is control. Being in effort is about operating from our head and not our heart. When we live in fear or don't trust that our lives will unfold in our best interests or to our highest good, we try to override the system by forcing outcomes. It's exhausting, and it doesn't work. After all, we are not in full control of our lives, so holding on too tightly is destined to be a failing strategy. In fact, the more we "effort," the more we unintentionally limit the outcome. To be clear, allowing things to happen is not the same as stepping back and doing nothing. We are each meant to put forth our best effort in Earth School. This means: showing up to class with the intention to learn and to do our fair share of the work.

Not long ago I did a reading for Laurie, a woman who'd lost her twenty-two-year-old son, Cooper, to a rare complication during a routine surgery. Cooper came through in spirit communicating that he'd left on a "high." At first, I thought to myself, this spirit has a twisted sense of humor. He's using a pun as a "sign," but I soon understood that Cooper wasn't referring to a high from anesthesia, but that his life was *on high*. He was engaged and soon to be married. He had a good job and was well liked by friends, family, and in his community. Because he was in such a good place, his early passing came as a shock to everyone, and his mother especially felt like death had come for the wrong guy. "Why would this happen," she wondered aloud, "when his future was so bright and promising?" Laurie was confused and deeply resentful.

I shared with her what Cooper was communicating with me. "Your son was excelling in Earth School, and even though he was young, he's showing me that it was time to go. He was 'complete.' I know it doesn't make sense and it doesn't feel fair, but it's not uncommon for people to die when they're on top. It means they did their work; they did their best and they passed their tests, and there isn't anyone or anything to blame for their death. Your son is showing me a street sign with two plates pointing in opposite directions. One represents trust and the other one points toward the lower frequencies of fear and doubt. Cooper is clearly pointing you in the direction of trust. In fact, his death is meant to help you learn and embody the meaning of trust and surrender." I cautiously shared the generational pattern I was seeing, like a family tree, its limbs stretching out in all directions. "You tend to control the events in your life. I see this in your mother, too. She didn't trust people, is that true?"

"My mother was brought up to 'trust no one but yourself,' and as a divorced, single, full-time working mom, I followed her lead; I've always been cautious with money and who I brought into Cooper's life."

"His death is to help you humbly reconcile the truth that you cannot control it all. It's going to take some time, but if you can loosen your grip around the details of 'how' he died, your grief will eventually loosen its grip on you."

Beliefs Have Energy

. . .

The narrative of having "bad luck" is a pervasive narrative in today's world. When we buy into this story line and let victim energy hijack our thoughts, feelings, words, and actions, we grow that feeling and attract more of it, like a mirror back on ourselves. This only reinforces our "bad luck" belief system, and the infinite loop of feeling powerless continues. In *Spirited*, I wrote about two types of people—Lucky and Unlucky. For the lucky person, life always seems to be working out. Lucky has financial stability, a great partner, a strong community, and is often upgraded to the hotel suite and released from jury duty at nine in the morning.

Unlucky, on the other hand, never wins anything. In fact, everything seems to go wrong for Unlucky—bad credit, a leaky roof, and one failed relationship after another.

What's the difference between the two? Not Luck. Lucky taps into the higher energetic frequencies of faith and trust and lives in a state of forgiveness for what *was* and in gratitude for what *is*. Rather than trying to control every aspect of her life, she lets her life unfold. Sure, she has struggles like the rest of us, but she looks for the lesson in every situation and how it may help her advance in Earth School.

My years of Spirit work tell me this is true: every challenge or hardship we face offers us an opportunity to grow our inner knowing that our lives are not random, unintentional, unfair, or even cruel. Unexpected turns like a health scare, a relationship betrayal, or a financial loss, for example, serve to shake us up and wake us up to an important lesson. And when we choose to unravel the lesson from the struggle, we stop feeling and living our lives as a victim of circumstance. Spirits come through in readings—every day!—to remind the living that the energetic vibration of our thoughts count, so if you're someone who'd rather identify with Lucky than Unlucky, let's get to work *right now* to change the narrative that you are a victim of your circumstances:

I am powerless ⇨

I AM empowered.
I AM remembering to have faith and trust.

Again, if embracing this new narrative feels hard for you, if you find yourself in resistance, thinking, *sounds great, but trust feels risky and unreliable*, then this is your clue that the old story you're telling yourself is deserving your attention. Don Miguel Ruiz writes in *The Four Agreements* that "awareness is always the first step because if you are not aware, there is nothing to change. If you are not aware that your mind is full of wounds and emotional poison, you cannot begin to clean and heal the wounds and you will continue to suffer."

Outlined on the following page are my favorite affirmations for growing the type of awareness Ruiz is talking about and imprinting this lesson on the heart to raise our energy.

When you feel doubtful and uncertain, repeat mentally or out loud:

- I trust that I AM here by design.
- I AM investing my faith and trust in Spirit and the greater plan.
- I AM connected to the truth that all is in perfect order.
- I AM the cocreator of my life.
- I AM remembering.
- I AM THAT I AM.

"I AM" are two of the most powerful words you can use to begin a sentence, wrote the late Wayne Dyer. "Anytime you start a sentence with I AM, you are creating what you are and what you want to be." Jose Luis Stevens extends this thought in *How to Pray the Shaman's Way*. "When you say I AM, you acknowledge that whatever you are stating is already true. I AM acknowledges what is so."

Since making the I AM THAT I AM mantra a regular habit in my life I've noticed that in addition to shifting my energy, it also serves to lift the energy around me. As I was writing this chapter in the spring of 2022, Russia had begun its brutal invasion of Ukraine. Day after day, I'd come home to find Chris and a handful of the kids glued to the television, watching the nightly news. As an empath who's highly intuitive, I'd immediately *feel* the heaviness of the situation, a total contrast to the high-vibe energy of the spirit world in which I spend the majority of my days. In general, I make it a point *not to* watch more than a few segments of the news, just enough to stay informed. After about twenty minutes, I have to unplug from the lower-vibe frequency, or my head will physically start to throb as I feel my energy slow down. I take this as my cue to exit stage right. On this night, the news was especially grim, and like so many of us, I became sucked into a dark place of fear and desperation. Before I got stuck, I retreated upstairs to my bedroom where I popped in my AirPods and cranked the solfeggio frequencies while chanting the I AM THAT I AM affirmations about faith and trust while mentally "running" gold energy from my crown to my heart center. I also took the opportunity to send out healing light for all those souls in the Ukraine who were actively experiencing or perpetuating darkness, fear, and struggle. After ten minutes, I felt an energetic lift and shift to my mood, and within moments my kids started entering my room one by one. It started with Haven, who crawled into bed with me and said, "I just want to be near you." Sam came next, "just to say 'hi,'" followed by Jakob, then Hadley, then Harper, who asked me random questions as they sprawled out on the bed. Finally, Chris joined in (and if Hannah weren't away at college, I bet she would have also piled on), and we suddenly started laughing at how we were all crammed into one room when we have a full house for the eight of us to spread out. It was a funny scene, and yet I knew exactly what was going on—my energy had drawn them in.

Exercise

* * * *

Wash Yourself with Violet

Flipping a belief and reframing it as a positive statement, mantra, or invocation is a powerful practice, and in addition to repeating the I AM mantra to align with the truth that there is a plan for your life at work behind the scenes, you will "run the color of violet" throughout your body. Within the shamanic tradition, violet vibrates at the frequency of forgiveness. Its frequency is incompatible with the low light of blame or judgment. You will run violet through your system to release this shadow energy of cynicism and distrust and to forgive yourself for any failed attempts to control the events of your life and resisting what is meant to be. Let the color violet spark trust that you are on the right path and that it is safe to surrender resentment and control.

Close your eyes and take several deep breaths to ground you in the present moment. Sit up straight with your feet on the ground and your hands resting in your lap. Pull your shoulder blades back and drop them down, and feel your chest push out and forward. Now, center your focus on the top of your head and visualize a door opening, or unscrewing a lid off a jar. Next, visualize a powerful violet light flooding down from up above like a waterfall descending into your crown chakra. Again, if visualization is a challenge for you, use your physical senses. Researcher Rikard Kuller discovered that when color is transmitted from the eye to the brain, it releases a hormone that affects our emotions, mind clarity, and energy levels. Try placing an amethyst crystal in your line of vision or a vase of violet-colored flowers. I will often turn on my LED floor lamp that rotates between different colors and stop on the color that I want to run through my energetic body. I focus on the light as I repeat my mantra and visualize that I am breathing in this color, allowing it to circulate throughout my body.

Once you have a mental picture or a visual representation of violet light pouring into your crown, descend it down into your heart center and lock it into place, as if you're dropping an anchor. Invite the violet light of truth to flow through your body and remind you of the I AM presence that exists within you, around you, and *is* you. As you "run your energy" with the color of violet, you will also tap on the meridian points from the diagram on page 78. Remember, tapping works to restore the balance of energy in your body and resolve low-frequency beliefs. In addition, there is undeniable power in the practice of repetition; it encodes whatever we're saying in our consciousness. As you tap on the "karate chop point," repeat any or all of the following statements three times. Choose the sentiments that most resonate with you or feel free to make up your own, either repeating the same or different statements each time.

- Even though I'm feeling fearful/disconnected/ungrounded . . . I AM here, willing and ready to receive an upgrade to my energy.
- Even though I'm feeling distrustful/suspicious/insecure/ unsafe . . . I AM trusting that my life is unfolding in Divine timing and order.
- Even though I'm feeling powerless and beaten down by life . . . I AM ready to shift my perspective and see my struggle as an opportunity to learn and grow.

- Even though I have lost faith and trust in the Divine plan
  . . . I accept where I AM right now.

After tapping on the "karate chop point," follow with a round of *feeling* statements that affirm the truth of how you feel. Remember: keep it simple. As you tap on the remaining eight meridian points—starting at the eyebrow point and ending at the top of the head—express an emotion that's got you down. It could be a single word . . . "lost," "powerless," "suspicious" . . . or even a single sound . . . "ugh" or a long exhale.

Follow this round with another full round of tapping on all eight meridian points, while repeating the I AM statements again:

- I AM here, willing and ready to receive an upgrade to my energy.
- I AM trusting that my life is unfolding in Divine timing and order.
- I AM ready to shift my perspective and see my struggle as an opportunity to learn and grow.
- I accept where I AM right now.

As you repeat the I AM statements, imagine that you are creating the *feeling* of trust, determination, and personal conviction that comes after the words *I AM*. Continue to breathe deeply, and don't be surprised if you start to feel a shift in your energy that you project out into the world.

Breathe IN: I AM. Breathe OUT: Empowered.

Before we move on, I want to pause and remind you that this is a practice that takes practice. If you don't feel an immediate shift in your energy, that's okay. It will take some time to get the hang of it, which is why you will be building on this homework assignment of changing the narrative and elevating your energy in every chapter.

Spirits often communicate that we do not open up to "remembering" our important life lessons all at once. Rather, it's a gradual process that can take a whole lifetime, and spirits applaud the living who do find the meaning, the rhyme, and the reason in their struggles while still in Earth School. Most of the spirits I talk to daily, excluding those ascended beings in the purple robes I mentioned earlier, are only *now* figuring it out on the Other Side.

As you continue to raise your energy through the repetition of I AM statements, tapping, and "running" colors, be patient with yourself. If tough feelings come up, remember to observe them as if they're resting in the palm of your hand. There are days when I get hung up on the first half of the I AM statements, and my energy stagnates. In the early lockdown days of Covid, especially, I had a hard time getting past "even though I'm feeling unsafe . . ." to the second part, "I AM trusting that my life is unfolding in Divine timing and order." If this also happens to you, try to be compassionate with yourself. Can you accept the hard feelings that come up, rather than turn away from and resist them? It's when we're in a surrendered state of feeling, rather than in fight-or-flight or escape mode, when true shifts and transformation can take place.

Follow the
Bread Crumbs

• • •

As you continue your practice of energy work, I encourage you to look for signs, or what I call bread crumbs, from Spirit. In the next chapter, I'll explore the many ways in which Spirit speaks to us, or at least tries to communicate with us, but for now, consider the familiar feeling of déjà vu—those flashback moments that make you feel like *I've been here before.* As I've come to understand it by way of a lucid dream in which my guides revealed its hidden meaning, déjà vu is Spirit impressing us with thoughts and feelings that are flashbacks of our prebirth plan and are meant to remind us that this moment in time, which may include select people, special details, and the specific place where you find yourself, is *playing out as planned, on purpose.* When it occurs, it's meant to inspire trust that you're on track and that your life is unfolding just as it was scripted. In other words, it's meant to be happening! Rather than doubt or question where you're at, have faith and keep following the bread crumbs.

Recently, a déjà vu moment played out in my own life when I was standing in the kitchen with my thirteen-year-old son, Sam, discussing his upcoming bar mitzvah. It was an ordinary moment, but I felt strongly like I was flashing back on a moment in time that I'd had before, sending a wave of chills up and down my arms. I knew what this meant—*everything was unfolding according to plan.* Let me back up—five days before this moment, I did not believe things were lining up or unfolding accordingly. In fact, we had gone into emergency "crunch mode" after I received a call from the rabbi and cantor, who expressed great concerns over Sam's readiness to stand on the pulpit and read from the Torah. During their most recent live rehearsal, they realized that Sam didn't actually know how to "read" Hebrew and was only reciting from memory. In doing so, he was making significant mistakes. It was an "Oh, shit moment," as Sam had been practicing with a tutor over the past several months on Zoom. But now, face-to-face with the Torah scroll, it was coming to light that he wasn't as prepared as we all had believed and expected. With only one week before several out-of-state family members were traveling in for the big event, Sam had a lot of work to do. Talk about leaving things to the eleventh hour! He crammed day and night up until my déjà vu moment in the kitchen, when I was reminded to get out of my head and into my heart and relax already, trust and be assured that events were unfolding according to plan. It took the edge off me, the nervous mother who'd been fretting that I'd have some big-time explaining to do if Sam bombed on his big day. Well, he didn't bomb. He pulled it off with grace and charm, reminding me that even when there appears to be strong evidence to the contrary, our lives are often perfectly on track.

Over the years, I've come to recognize that déjà vu moments are sprinkled into our lives to get our attention, as in, *Hey, heads-up, this matters!* They're meant to awaken our trust when we are questioning our current situation or when we can't make heads or tails of our struggle. The next time you have a déjà vu moment, rather

than question or dismiss it, can you open up to the *feeling* of familiarity and trust that this moment in your life is happening exactly
as planned?

Grow the Feeling through Inspired Action

• • •

You don't have to wait for déjà vu moments to grow your trust.
My favorite way to "test fate" is to follow my gut, that is, my
intuition. I liken intuition to an internal GPS system—it tells
us where we are and where we need to go in life. Others refer
to intuition as your inner voice, innate wisdom, gut knowing,
instinct, sixth sense, a hunch, or simply "the feels." However you
refer to it, intuition is our most powerful tool. We're all born
with it, yet most of us don't take full advantage of it because
we lack trust, in ourselves, in others, in the things we cannot
see, in the bigger picture unfolding behind the scenes. We want
"proof" when the clarity we seek is within reach. When you are
able to quiet your mind and listen to your true feelings, you
can better navigate your life without all the over-efforting and
control. When we trust the guidance we receive and act on it—
and it is validated!—our trust goes through the roof, expanding
exponentially each time we act on it.

The following story about my mom, Jan Goldstein, is one my
brothers and I heard countless times growing up as a cautionary
reminder to listen to our intuition and to trust that it is meant to

both guide and protect us and to bolster our trust in the bigger plan for our lives. Rather than rewrite Mom's story from memory, I asked her to share it in her own words.

It was 1964 and I was in the tenth grade. I lived in Woodland Hills, in the west end of the San Fernando Valley in California. My friends and I were just starting to become young adults, getting our driver's permits, and our primary focus was on having fun and hanging out at the beautiful beaches that were just on the other side of Topanga Canyon, which was popularized through songs by The Mamas & The Papas and frequented by The Beach Boys (yes, The Beach Boys), who played at nearby venues. These were the days when you'd see Sonny & Cher driving down Ventura Boulevard, and Ike and Tina Turner were playing at local hangouts. Our entire existence was about getting to the beach, typically with older friends who could shuttle us over the hill and back. We were good kids. We didn't drink or do drugs. Our "bad" behavior fell under the category of harmless pranks or coming home an hour late after curfew. One morning, a friend had the idea to sneak out early on a Saturday to do a surf ride and watch the sunrise. A group of five came to my house at three in the morning, and I quietly slipped out the back door and went with them. I felt like what I was doing was wrong, but I went anyway, and the sunrise was beautiful. Still, I was nervous that my parents would wake up and discover me gone and worry about me. Thankfully, I was back home before Dad even woke up. We'd pulled off our caper, so naturally, the following Saturday, this same group of friends wanted to do it all over again, but when they tapped on my bedroom window at

3:00 A.M., I waved them away. I knew it was wrong for me to sneak out and lie to my parents. I'd done it once, and I wasn't going to do it again. They drove off and I went back to sleep.

Later that morning, I vividly recall my sister answering a phone call. It was from my friend Sandy's mom. Did I know anything about the accident in Topanga Canyon? Sandy and four of my friends were in the hospital. Did I know anything about it? I arrived at the hospital and learned that my friend Sam, who was underage and driving, lost control going around a curve at a hundred miles per hour. The car had crashed into the hillside.

Sam was unconscious, his face unrecognizable; my girlfriend Sandy was also unconscious, and her right eye was severely damaged; our friend Beth had a broken arm and leg, and Mike still suffers to this day with resulting issues from the crash. Everyone was alive, but the experience physically and mentally impacted each of them in profound ways.

When I tearfully confessed to my parents that we'd been sneaking out of our homes and driving out to the beach, my father took me to see the car, which was smashed like a pancake. It had been towed into a small gas station. He made me look at the steering wheel, where teeth were implanted, and the jagged glass windshield splattered with hair and blood. He did not want me to forget that I, too, could have been in that crash.

So, what did I take away from that experience? I learned that every day and at every point in our lives, we are faced with choices. What do we do? Do we listen to the voice inside? What is that voice telling us? Are we acting from that voice? The first time I snuck out of my house, I dismissed the voice that said 'this is wrong.' I made a reckless choice. The second time, I listened to my intuition, and the right choice just may, and very probably did, save my life. We can lie to our parents—that's not okay. But when we lie to ourselves, that's really not okay. The valuable lesson I learned that day was to listen to and honor your inner voice. Trust it and trust that there is a plan.

Your homework assignment before moving on to the next chapter is to use small opportunities to grow your intuition. As a suggestion, the next time you are on the road, ask your intuition to lead the way. Now, I don't suggest that you simply get in your car and let your intuition take the wheel, but that you pay attention to your intuition as you're driving. Spirits have shared with me that "drive time" can be an optimal time not only to receive messages from beyond, but also to tune in to your intuition. This is because we're often engaged in the present moment when we're behind the wheel, and our presence creates a window to the unseen, like putting on magic sunglasses. It might sound like hocus-pocus, but it comes back to energy: when you can tune in to the higher vibrational channel of your own intuition, the radio static disappears, and the answers become clear.

So, the next time you hit the road, tune in to your intuition, and invite it to speak directly to you through your feelings. Also be on alert for how your intuition delivers information through insights, revelations, and urges, including definitive yes and no answers. As an example, I want to include my own driving story as a pickup to my mom's.

Not too long ago, I was in the market for a new car. I'd turned in the lease to my existing car eight months early for a reimbursement check ($12k!), which was a wonderful windfall, but it left me driving a rental car indefinitely. As I was driving the rental to work one morning, I asked my guides to help me with my car situation, and almost as soon as I asked for guidance, I passed two cars with license plates containing the number sequence 268, which is my own numeric sign for "trust your intuition." No sooner had I noted the plates when I glanced down at my mileage and nearly hit the brakes when I read 268 miles on the odometer. Three times is a charm, and it definitely got my attention.

As guided, I tuned in to my intuition throughout the day and I started to *feel* that there was a car out there, waiting for me right *now*, despite the supply chain backlog, which I knew was a reality. Custom car orders were taking a minimum of three months to fill, and the last time I checked, there was limited availability on dealership lots. Still, I suggested to Chris that we go car shopping just in case, or at least for fun.

That weekend we hit three different dealerships, and within minutes of walking through the limited inventory, I knew none of the vehicles were right for me and finally concluded, "I'd rather wait for the right car than settle on something today." We were about to head home when Chris suggested, "How bout we check out just one more dealership?"

"Okay, sure," I relented. "Why not?"

As we pulled into a smaller dealership off the beaten path, a tow truck with the word *SHELL* on its side was pulling out. Shel was my dad's nickname, and seeing it made me smile. "Hi, Dad," I said quietly to myself.

As we walked into the dealership, the salesperson apologized that they had only one car that fit my criteria. It was a floor model, preowned but with very low mileage and at a great price. And it was available now. As soon as I saw it, I knew it was the one. Without hesitation, I said, "I'll take it!"

The sale was seamless and easy, and the next day when I returned the rental car, I noticed that the daily rate had been $26.80! Add to that, when I checked out, my total bill came to, you guessed it—$268.00

As I drove my new car later that day, I felt a swell of gratitude for all the signs I'm afforded from the Other Side and for my Team Spirit intervening on my behalf to make my life unfold with ease. That said, I know that this particular unfolding wouldn't have happened had I not trusted my intuition and the process. Since getting my new car, my guides have shown me in meditation that it's meant to serve as a physical and daily reminder to trust that my life is unfolding according to plan. And when in doubt, to ask for and then look for the signs.

When we remember that Spirit has a plan for our lives that we can access through our intuition, our days start to flow with more ease and less distraction, as if we're cruising down an open road with nothing but sky for miles ahead. To access your open road plan, ask for guidance and then express heartfelt gratitude in advance that you will receive it. Say: *Thank you Spirit, angels, and guides for reminding me of your presence already with me. Thank you for the clear guidance.* Putting positive emotion behind your request is key because—I've said it before—emotion is energy in motion, contracting and expanding, producing its own vibration and frequency. When you offer gratitude ahead of time, Spirit can more easily fulfill your request because it tunes into and responds to higher frequencies like love and gratitude. By creating a daily practice of connecting with both your intuition and with Spirit, you will call into your life your most heartfelt hopes, needs, and desires.

CHAPTER 5

I AM Supported;
I AM Surrounded

. . .

I take my work very seriously. I feel that it's my responsibility to
show up for others because I recognize that what I do is more
than a job; it's my soul's purpose. After years of doing my own
homework, I am being called to share my notes, to be of service to
people like you who are tackling your own assignments. And for
this reason, I rarely, if ever, cancel readings at the last minute. On a
recent morning, however, I had no choice. I canceled a full sched-
ule of readings when I woke up feeling so awful that I could hardly
drag myself out of bed. I was certain I had Covid, again, but three
negative tests suggested otherwise. I collapsed back into bed with
full-body aches, a throbbing headache, and my stomach in knots.
If not Covid, then what was ailing me? A series of bloodwork and
lab tests later that week confirmed the presence of the Epstein-
Barr virus (the most common cause of infectious mononucleosis
or "mono"), mold, yeast, and bacteria toxicity. It was a witch's brew

of digestive issues that weren't life-threatening but still made me very uncomfortable. My doctor put me on a protocol of dozens of natural supplements to release the toxins, cleanse my organs, and restore digestive order. But I still wasn't able to flush the toxins out of my system. I was reabsorbing them, which caused me to feel sick and sluggish all over again. That's when I knew I needed next-level support. I asked for guidance, and I was shown what was happening underneath my physical pain. I was emotionally and spiritually drained.

Of course I was.

Once again, I wasn't walking my talk. I hadn't been setting healthy boundaries in my work and home life. I was allowing myself to absorb and hold everyone's energy at my own expense. I immediately recognized this over-giving and overextending trait because I observe it in so many of the clients I counsel, especially those who are natural empaths and caretakers like me, who unconsciously ignore their own need for self-care. In readings, their deceased loved ones encourage them to "pull their energy back" or suffer the consequences: burnout. I know this well, and still I wasn't following the guidance. I was over-efforting in an attempt to do and *be* it all for my clients, my family, and my friends. And guess what happens when you hold tightly on to control like it's the last life preserver on the boat? You get constipated.

"You're holding everyone's shit" is how my bestie Laura bluntly described it.

My energy healer, Jakki, confirmed this in less colorful terms. She said, "Your body cannot metabolize all the energy you're holding of the living and the dead. I'm also seeing ancestral lineage stuff that you're carrying around, energy that's not yours that's causing you to feel anxious and afraid. This external energy is clogging you up and slowing you down on every level. You feel drained because you are!"

Jakki's and Laura's insights felt right. Later that day in meditation, I asked for more clarification, and *get this*: a stalk of celery and a lemon wedge appeared in my mind's eye. Long story short, it was the message I needed to finally try a juicing protocol my friends had been raving about. I hadn't wanted to devote the time and energy before, but now I was willing to try anything.

A couple of weeks later, I woke up feeling like a new person. I jumped out of bed while noting the time, 6:28 A.M. This number is my birthday, June 28, and spirits will often use this numeric sequence to get my attention. I took it as my "sign" that I was on the right path. That day, my readings were noticeably clear and spot on, and my energy had returned to its full capacity.

I share this story as my humble admission that even I get stuck. Even I bypass my heart and listen to my head, even though I know better, to the point of making myself sick. As you continue to build and trust your intuition, your inner GPS system, give yourself some grace when you intentionally drive off-road and let your mind take the wheel. We're culturally conditioned to listen to our mind chatter and to follow its persuasive lead, but our best guidance comes through our intuition, our hearts. When we learn to listen to and trust our hearts, we build confidence in our inner knowing. It's through our hearts that we also receive signs and confirmation that we are not alone.

This is Lesson 3: I AM supported; I AM surrounded.

I know all too well how difficult it can be to admit that we cannot do it all, handle it all, hold it all, control it all. We are each an effective and powerful resource, but we are not all powerful on our own, nor are we the ultimate energy source. So many of us learn this lesson the hard way (guilty!), letting our energy reserves run out until they eventually burn out, distrusting that we can release our firm grip on life because of the high value our culture places on individualism, so often displayed by the pervasive "I've got this!" mentality. The feelings that accompany this cycle are uncertainty and overwhelm which align with low-level energy.

Help, I Need Somebody

• • •

I met Stacy after she'd experienced her own rapid unfolding, both personally and professionally. She explained that she'd always been a "doer"—first for her parents and siblings, and then in her marriage and her work running a medium-size architectural firm. But after a decade and a half of doing, ramping up to three kids and two dozen employees, Stacy's ability to "do" had stretched to and beyond capacity. Her relationships with both her husband and the business partner she referred to as her "work husband" were strained for lack of support, her elementary school–age kids were acting out for want of time with her, and she began and ended her days in a house that seemed to be in a constant state of irretrievable mess.

"I look like I have it together, but I feel trapped—tethered to this overwhelming path. I want to course-correct for myself, for my family, and for my work, but I don't know how." She summed up her situation this way: "I've always been the one to say, 'Don't worry, I'll take care of it,' but now *I need help*, and I don't know where to get it."

Stacy described herself as the "I'll take care of it" person in her family, and as she spoke, I could feel her fear and overwhelm in the pit of my stomach. I'd recently learned the term "high-functioning codependency," which describes people who prioritize the needs and desires of others over their own, either because they fear losing control or they fear being abandoned if they don't prove themselves useful to those around them.

Stacy's spirit guide stepped forward to show me a mental movie of her childhood. I understood through my own frame of reference to my childhood experience of living with a strong paternal presence that Stacy had also grown up with a narcissistic father who demanded attention and who taught her from an early age that it wasn't safe to voice her own needs; it was safer to "play Mommy" and ensure others' needs were met in order to avoid conflict, but at the price of denying whatever she needed from her home life and her friendships. As an adult, she'd unconsciously taken on a motherly role with both her husband and her male business partner, by doing more than her fair share of the household and professional workload which, over time, enabled them both to do even less. The men in Stacy's life had relied on her to be the "doer" to her detriment, but hadn't years together taught them that this was acceptable to Stacy?

"You've created a habit of putting everyone else first *at your own expense*," I told her. "You're forgetting yourself entirely. Sure it worked when you were a girl, but once you added your own house, kids, and an office full of other adults who required your attention, the self-forgetting became *too expensive*—emotionally, physically, and quite literally financially. Now you have nothing left to give to yourself or anyone else. Now *you* need the help, and you need to trust that you can ask for it without being rejected. And, that you *will* get it," I said.

Stacy rolled her eyes. "Good luck. My husband and my business partner are incapable of rising to the occasion."

"You're right," I agreed. "Their support falls short. What I'm telling you is that you're being called to seek help *elsewhere*, from a more reliable source. From Spirit."

I told Stacy that I clairvoyantly "saw" her making a big move, one that would restore her energy reserves. "They're not showing me the details," I admitted, "only that change is in the works."

Six months later, I heard from Stacy that she had moved across the country to be closer to her parents, where she started a new business independent of her work husband. And she'd done so without her legal husband. She also began a daily spiritual practice of meditation to connect with her intuition, and on my recommendation, she'd started working with an energy healer. She wrote in an email to me:

After our reading, I went into triage mode and started meditating every morning, quite literally speaking to my guides, begging for guidance, courage, and strength to carry me through that day, that week and month, to please deliver me safely to the other side of what I regarded as a terrifying separation from all that I'd known before, that path that I felt trapped by. Taking a step every day to move further away from that trajectory was my 'dark night of the soul.' During this daily morning ritual, I visualized my future self and how I wanted my life to look and *feel* like when I was free of the stress, conflict, and struggle. I would 'call in' this vision, asking for it to become my present reality. And you know what? It *did* become my reality. Little by little, small changes created bigger and bigger shifts. My kids felt it, too, and observing them, I could feel their collective exhale as they leaned back into calmer versions of themselves right alongside me. Today this is my reality. Nothing's perfect, of course, but I no longer feel out of control . . . and I live in an orderly house, that's for sure!

But more importantly, now *I get it.* I trust that I can ask, and I *will* get the help that I need, because I'm asking from the right helper—not a husband or a business partner, but from my 'team in spirit,' who are my real partners irrespective of who else I stand or work beside. These days this asking is second nature to me, though my morning practice serves as a daily reminder, and I never feel alone—I know my team is with me throughout the day. Often, I'll pause before a tough call and say, 'Please be with me,' or 'Please tell me what to do here,' and I trust the intuition that follows. And this includes the guidance that keeps me working to 'own' my part in how I *chose* to set up my relationships—with my family and kids, my colleagues and clients—and also the ways in which I fail to make room for reciprocity by over-doing. As I have released the people in my life who could not or would not reciprocate based on my over-doing or otherwise, healthier relationships and work projects were able to come in.

So many of the people I counsel and support express sentiments like Stacy's:

It's all on me.

I feel overwhelmed.

I can't do it all.

If I stop holding it all together, my world will fall apart.

I feel alone.

I feel burdened.

I feel lost.

I feel afraid.

I don't know what step to take next.

I get it. I feel the fear and can be overwhelmed, too, and before you take your next step forward, I offer you the same advice I give myself—

Ask for help.

So many of us white-knuckle our way through life, feeling like we're on our own as we navigate every turn, unaware of the guidance that is available when we ask for it. An unseen support system is available to direct, comfort, and protect every one of us through life's ups and downs. Yes, *every one of us.* I've served as a medium between this world and the next for more than two decades, and still, I'm no different from you. We all have a team on the Other Side.

In addition to prearranging our biggest lessons before being born, our Council of Elders helps us assemble a team of spiritual beings to guide us through Earth School, akin to selecting your favorite professors before the term begins. Over the years, I've relied on these light beings to help me make solid and irrefutable connections for thousands of men and women desperately seeking answers, resolution, and validation that they are not alone when trying to figure it all out. It's the same support system that I personally rely on when I'm plagued with uncertainty and doubt and wish for clarity. On any given day, I call on my team of deceased loved ones, personal spirit guides, healing masters, and angels with a heavenly perspective to send me signs, provide me with insights, and line up synchronistic events throughout my day to help support and guide me in the best direction forward. My ask is simple: show me the next steps. Just like you, I want reassurance that my hardships and struggles have a rhyme and a reason. I want resolution around particular situations. And sometimes, I need to be reminded of what I already intuitively know. While I have a heightened sensitivity and a natural knack for this type of spirit communication, you, too, can connect with your Team Spirit. You can learn to recognize messages and "signs" to better understand how your day-to-day life experience fits into the bigger picture.

It's magical stuff, and I'm excited to share all that I know, but before we talk about how to connect, let's review all the players on your team.

Team Spirit

Every day, you are surrounded by your own Team Spirit—deceased loved ones, personal guides, and angelic helpers and healers who are waiting in eager anticipation to work with and assist you. They each play different roles and have varied areas of expertise. Consider them your teachers here in Earth School:

Archangels

In their purest form, angels are highly evolved spiritual beings of divine light, and because their energy is so light, bright, and spinning off the charts, they cannot physically be contained in a human body. The archangels hold the highest rank in the angelic realm because they are the most evolved. They're who you want to call on when you need powerful, immediate help.

Guardian Angels

We each have one or two dedicated guardian angels that have assisted us from the day we were born and are committed to guide and protect us until the day we die. In fact, before we were each born, we chose our guardian based on the lessons, obstacles, and goals we set up for ourselves. Because of this, our guardians are very familiar with our "soul contract" and take it as their responsibility to keep us on track, steering us in the direction of the path of least resistance and toward the doors that will open the greatest opportunities for learning in our lives. Our guardians *feel* us and have the ability to intervene in our lives if we're in danger. They also serve as the touch point for all other "team" members to determine what type of help you need at a particular moment or period of your life.

Angels

These golden beings of light act as helper angels to all people, responding to our general calls for guidance, comfort, or support. They can also step in to help us with specific situations, like finding a new home or job. They are dedicated to service with unlimited time and energy (can you imagine?) and are available to us at all times. Angels like to send us signs and arrange synchronistic events to let us know that we're on the right path.

Ascended Masters

Where angels were never in a human body, the ascended masters did previously walk the Earth as powerful healers, prophets, or mentors (such as Jesus, Mother Mary, Quan Yin, Buddha, Mother Teresa, and St. Francis of Assisi). After their physical lifetimes, they graduated to a much higher level of being, where they continue to act in service to humanity without returning to Earth School.

Spirit Guides

Spirit guides are enlightened spirits who have completed a lot of advanced classes, and now they're available to share what they've learned with the living. Our individual spirit guides frequently work in tandem with our deceased loved ones to support us through challenging periods of our lives, although we've rarely known or met these spirits in human form. In general, spirit guides tend to be between lifetimes, taking a break from physical life, and they "drop in" with us at different times of our life, depending on the lesson or assignment we are learning, much like having a variety of teachers focused on different course material. Their role is to assist us, not rescue us from our challenges. Whether it's healing from a divorce, surviving the first year of motherhood, or managing a career change, your guides may inspire you to move in a particular direction or make a difficult decision, or simply surround you with their loving energy to help you feel supported and less alone. Our guides come and go throughout our lifetime as we graduate from one assignment to the next. Once they sense our work is done in a particular area, they move on to help someone else.

Deceased Loved Ones

Your deceased loved ones don't have the awesome powers of your guardian angels or the wisdom of the ascended masters, and yet they step in as our most enthusiastic cheerleaders and serve to support us as much as they're able. At some point, a deceased loved one may become a guide, much like my grandma Babe, but not until they complete their own work and undergo extensive training to responsibly assist the living. Most often, our deceased loved ones will reach out across the divide to simply say hello and remind you that they're still with you; they're never truly gone. They're surrounding you with love and light every day.

Incarnated Beings of Light

No matter their actual age, these are the people you meet who seem wise and insightful beyond their years, like they've "done" life before. Think of these old souls as high-achieving students who graduated magna cum laude in the spirit world and are now back for more. These high-vibe people have incarnated before, and this time around, they're here to serve humankind and the planet. They may die young or from a tragic event that serves to teach someone else a valuable lesson or to heal and uplift a community.

Animal Guides

Both alive and in spirit form, animal energy is angelic. Our pets, specifically, serve to provide us with unconditional love and tend to sense when we are struggling. Their light and bright energy also help to elevate our own by activating our hearts to be open to receiving and giving love. Animal guides will sometimes appear in our dreams or in daily life. Take notice of the animals that cross your path and wander into your yard.

Ground Crew

Your ground crew includes your living family and friends who are on assignment with you, and from whom you learn, and also teach, important life lessons.

Q: With so many spirits on the "team," how do I know who to call?

A: As you build this relationship, keep it simple. Call on your Team Spirit and leave it at that. No need to specify because the beings that can best support you will come forward. When I was struggling in college with depression, I prayed for something, anything, *anyone* to help me. My request was broad and uncomplicated. At the time, I didn't know who I was praying to; I just knew that I needed help, and my grandma Babe, along with my guardian angel, Maya, answered the call. Over time and through the process of automatic writing that I shared earlier, I was able to identify the spirits that were supporting me. As you become more familiar with the process of calling on your team, you may also be able to identify the spirits who are surrounding you. You may ask them their names or how they reveal themselves to you, either by a color, a sound, word, image, object, symbol, or a clear feeling. Tune in to their gender, it can be male, female, or neither. You may ask them what lessons they are here to help you learn. For now, don't overcomplicate it. Just ask.

Change the Narrative

• • •

So many of us journey through our lives unaware of or disbelieving that support and guidance is available as soon as we ask for it.

Let's change the narrative that leaves you feeling overwhelmed and undersupported:

I am on my own to figure it out. ⇨

I AM supported. I AM surrounded.

We're never alone throughout this human experience. We each have a team, a powerful group of spiritual beings working on our behalf behind the scenes. Every step of the way, they are watching, listening, and available to assist us at any time. We only need to ask. Without your permission, however, they will remain in the shadows. Due to the law of free will, your Team Spirit requires your invitation to step forward. And the more intentional, the better. Speak it out loud. Write it down, as if you're sending a formal party invite with an RSVP request. Sound the alarms, like you're paging the doctor. If you don't press the button, they won't come running. While this may sound like an *over-ask*, understand that spirits don't always hear us when we're feeling low because they're bouncing around at a much higher frequency. To get their attention and bring them down to our level, place your call without hesitation and with clear intention.

Exercise

Wash Yourself with Violet and Gold

What I've come to understand after working for more than two decades with enlightened spiritual beings is that our invitation needn't be formal; our heartfelt intention is enough because spirits *feel* us, and they feel the intention behind the words. This is another good reason to get out of our heads and into our hearts because it is within the energetic space of our hearts that we connect to Spirit, and the physical location of our invitation is not important, either. Lead with your heart, wherever you are.

This next exercise combines changing the narrative with an invitation to your team to step forward and surround you. As you raise your energy through visualization, you naturally become more aligned with the higher frequency of Spirit, sometimes referred to as "matching the frequency of miracle consciousness," and it is here that we receive guidance from beyond.

Start by closing your eyes. Take several deep breaths to ground you into your physical body in the present moment. Continue to breathe in and out slowly. Once your mind has had a moment to quiet down, visualize a swirl of violet and golden light a few feet above your head. With your next breath, draw this brilliant healing light down into the crown of your head, and farther down into your forehead and temples, into your cheeks and jaw. Let everything start to relax and soften as the swirl of violet and gold light releases any low-level energy associated with the belief that you are alone when navigating your life.

Allow the light to break apart energetic blocks of suffering and pain that is yours or that you are carrying for others. Feel it dissolve now.

As the light flows farther down into your heart, let it awaken the I AM presence that exists within you, around you, and *is* you. As you "run your energy" with the swirl of violet and gold, tap on the meridian points from the diagram on page 78. As you tap on the "karate chop point", repeat any or all of the following statements three times. Choose the sentiments that most resonate with you or feel free to make up your own, either repeating the same or different statements each time.

- Even though I'm feeling fearful . . . I AM supported. I open my heart to the guidance of a support system bigger than me.
- Even though I'm feeling alone and overwhelmed by the challenges and responsibilities of life . . . I AM surrounded. I AM calling on my Team Spirit to guide and support me.
- Even though I am feeling doubtful . . . I AM asking for clarity, insight, and trust.

After tapping on the "karate chop" point, follow with a round of *feeling* statements that affirm the truth of how you feel. As you tap on the remaining eight meridian points—starting at the eyebrow point and ending at the top of the head—express an emotion. It could be a single word . . . "fearful," "overwhelmed," "doubtful" . . . or even a single sound or a long exhale.

Follow this round with another full round of tapping on all eight meridian points, while repeating the I AM statements again:

- I AM supported. I open my heart to the guidance of a
support system bigger than me.
- I AM surrounded. I AM calling on my Team Spirit to guide
and support me.
- I AM asking for clarity, insight, and trust.

As you repeat the I AM statements while tapping, imagine that you are creating the *feeling* of trust and certainty that comes after the words *I AM*.

Continue to breathe IN: I AM. Breathe OUT: Surrounded and supported.

Now, with your heart open and with loving intention, call in your Team Spirit—your deceased loved ones, guides, and angels. Visualize the swirl of violet and gold light expanding outward, sending a swell of gratitude and deep appreciation for their unconditional love and presence in your life.

You may say: thank you for attuning my energy to the higher vibrational frequencies of Spirit. Help me to keep my heart open to receive your energy and guidance.

Next, ask your team to communicate with you with physical and mental signs, through dreams, insights, and by orchestrating synchronicities.

You may say: I invite you to show me clear signs of your presence in my life. I invite you to surround me so that I *feel* and *know* your presence. I welcome you to come forward at this time.

Take a few moments now to be still and receptive to messages from your team. Whatever guidance, visions, signs, or feelings that rise up within you, regard them with curiosity. Observe them, feel them, and trust them, if you can, and vow to remain aware and open to receiving signs from this day forward.

When you feel ready, bring your awareness back to your heart center and remember that at any moment you may invite your Team Spirit to show up as validation that you are connected and supported from beyond.

Grow the Feeling through Active Listening

• • •

If you didn't receive any big insights or "signs" on your first attempt, try again. Spirit communication takes practice, especially in a world where external turbulence easily disrupts inner reception. Amid the noise of everyday life and the internal mind chatter, it can be challenging to turn down the volume and listen to the still, open space within your heart: your intuition. It is necessary, however, to do this. To receive communication, we each must attune to our intuition, to our feelings. This is the channel that Spirit comes through.

My intuition plays a pivotal role in my mediumship work, and I've learned through much trial and error that *trust* and *listening* are essential to the practice. The first step is to suspend doubt, if only momentarily, but long enough to lean in to and trust your feelings. With trust in hand, it is equally important to listen to the varied ways your intuition speaks to you. When I'm trying to get a clear read on something, I will often ask myself: How does this situation *feel*? If I feel a physical contraction in my belly, that's my "sign" for STOP, it's a red light. Don't go forward. If, on the other hand, I feel a sense of expansion or lightness in reaction to my question, I take that as a green light to GO, to move ahead. I have learned that by quieting my mind and getting into a neutral headspace where I can truly listen, I will—and do—receive the clarity and guidance I'm seeking. Remember, spirits communicate through our intuition by way of our senses—what we're feeling, sensing, hearing, and seeing. Depending on your individual strengths and learning style, pay attention to the information you are receiving through all of your sensory channels, as well as your claircognizance, or gut feeling of *knowing*.

QUESTIONS FROM THE FRONT ROW

Q: What is a "sign" and how will I know if I've gotten one?
A: Our Team Spirit communicates with us through physical and mental signs. Physical signs relate to external phenomenon, such as interfering with electronics and technology, manipulating music and photography, influencing animals and birds, placing objects in our path, getting our attention with recurring number combinations, words, phrases, and special symbols. Our Team Spirit can also orchestrate synchronistic events like getting an unexpected tax refund for the exact amount of money you need, or changing your seat number on a flight so that you end up sitting next to the person who will become your future husband or wife. Both true stories told to me by clients, by the way!

A mental sign relates to internal phenomenon communicated through meditation, dream visitations, inspired thoughts and intuitive hits, déjà vu moments, and through channeled messages and automatic writing. The way in which a spirit attempts to connect depends on their level of evolution. The more evolved, the higher their aptitude and skill. Spirits also consider the "sign" that will most resonate with and capture our attention. Because of the many varied ways spirits try to get our attention, stay open to whatever shows up and trust that you'll know it when you see it.

Q: When I get a sign, how will I know who sent it?

A: Again, knowing who or what type of light being is delivering the message isn't imperative. But if you're curious, just ask. *Who are you? What message do you have for me? What do you want to teach me? How will I know it's you?* Set your intention to connect with your team through meditation, dreams, walking in nature, writing to them, or talking out loud to them. Do what feels right to you, and with practice, you will start to feel the difference in their energy just as we do with the people in our lives. For example, my dad's presence always feels subtle and soft, gentle, and wise, like he's standing in the corner of the room, not wanting to interrupt but quietly letting me know he's there if needed. (His presence in spirit contrasts to how he presented in life, *commanding and in charge*, but his many years of hard work on the Other Side have softened him.) Another one of my current spirit guides feels like a force to be reckoned with. In meditation, this spirit appears by my side with a sense of fierce strength, encouraging me to set boundaries and step into my full power. Like humans, different spirits give off different vibes. Once you start paying attention, the differences in how they feel and what they're here to help you with will become more clear.

Give Me Proof

• • •

It's easy to say—just trust and believe and that's when you'll begin to see the signs—but I understand that you may want tangible evidence, concrete examples of what I'm talking about here, so I've included several snapshot moments from people who came to me for readings and generously agreed to share their stories:

The day Kaitlin's brother Nick died, she had a dream visitation from him where he drew the outline of a heart, in the air, with his hands, and told her, *It's going to be okay, I love you.* Months later, at the time of our reading, Nick's spirit confirmed that he would send her hearts as a symbol of his eternal love. Fast forward to the first family vacation without him that summer when Kaitlin found a heart-shaped necklace in her hotel room. It wasn't hers; she hadn't noticed it until the last day of the trip, and yet suddenly, it appeared.

Gwen's husband, Marcus, loved hats. After his sudden death, she put his favorite hat away in the closet because it was too difficult for her to look at it. At the time of our reading, he communicated by flashing a visual in my mind's eye of him throwing or moving things around the house, and that he would leave things out "in plain sight" for Gwen to recognize and know that he was still present with her. When she returned home from the reading, his favorite hat was out of the closet and in the middle of their bedroom floor.

During my reading with Cynthia, her spirit guides inspired me to pass on this message: "They're saying that it's time to incorporate more joy into your busy life." She laughed and pulled up a picture on her phone of a license plate that read: BE JOYOUS. "Just two days ago," Cynthia shared, "I saw this license plate and felt compelled to take a picture of it. Now I know why."

Pop Quiz
A Sign or Making Things Fit?

YES, IT'S A SIGN

Music: Your deceased loved one's favorite song was "Hotel California" and as you're driving around and missing them, the song starts playing in the car without any prompting by you. Signs often appear after a recent conversation or while thinking about a deceased loved one.

Side note: After writing this little anecdote about "Hotel California," which just popped into my head, I had to leave the office for an appointment downtown. In the downstairs parking garage, I got into my car and fired up the GPS, and it wouldn't connect. I tried again and again and again. After three failed attempts, I took a deep breath and asked my Team Spirit for help, and then it hit me—turn off the Bluetooth on my phone, which I did, and it disconnected my phone from the car, which switched it to my car radio. Can you guess what was playing? "HOTEL CALIFORNIA"!!! I laughed and tried to reload the map, and it appeared immediately. On my drive to the meeting, I thanked my guides for their clever validation and for working behind the scenes to co-write this section on "signs" with me and for *you*.

Reading: You randomly flip open to a page in a book and your eyes lock in on a word, sentence, or passage that has meaning to your current situation or answers a specific question you've been asking. It's a sign; Spirit inspired you to pick up and read the right material at the right time. Your Team Spirit recognizes that you're highly clairvoyant, in addition to being an avid reader. Using a visual sign to get your full attention is the path of least resistance and the easiest way to communicate a message to you.

Electronics: You're trying to send a text or place a phone call and it won't go through. There is no explanation for why your phone isn't working, and you become frustrated and go into over-efforting, control mode. It still doesn't work, and you eventually give up. You try again a day later, and you're connected right away. Your "team" may have been warning you that the timing of this call or interaction was wrong. Perhaps you or the person you were trying to reach were not in the right frame of mind to send or receive your message.

Driving: A car cuts in front of you or parks behind you on the street with a personalized license plate that has special meaning to you. In a low-mood moment the other day, I asked my guides to help shift my energy, and less than a minute later, a car pulled in front of me with the license plate: GOODNRG (good energy).

NO, IT'S NOT A SIGN

Music: You were just listening to your favorite Spotify playlist and thinking about your deceased loved one. Suddenly, that person's favorite song—"Hotel California"—starts playing! A nice reminder of your loved one, yes, but not a sign. At some point, this was bound to happen, as it was initiated by you and is part of your curated playlist.

Reading: You're seeking an answer to something weighing heavily on you, so you go online and start researching the topic, only to find the exact information you need to read in this moment to help you solve the problem at hand. Handy and helpful, but not a sign. You manipulated the search and naturally found the material, no big surprise.

Electronics: Your cell phone drops a call. Unexpected, maybe, but not a sign. Sometimes we are in an area with poor reception and our screens go dark.

Driving: You walk out to your parked car on the street and there's a car with a license plate parked in front of you that has a vanity plate that, while interesting, means nothing special to you. Not a sign, sometimes a vanity plate is just that—a plate! In another instance, you have asked, specifically, for a sign on a license plate to provide you with guidance. As you pull into your office driveway, you notice a parked car with a meaningful plate. It feels like the sign you are looking for, however, it's a car that you routinely see every day. Not a sign.

Not everything you see, hear, or feel is going to be a sign from beyond. How then do you discern between a true "sign" and when you're making things fit? As a rule, learning how to read the signs becomes easier when you are able to distinguish between a mind thought and an intuitive thought. A mind thought is a trailed thought, where you think of something, which leads to another thought, and another and another until you've convinced yourself that you've arrived at the truth. For example: you're writing your to-do list for the day and add "call Sarah" to the list, remembering your friend's upcoming doctor's appointment. As you think further about Sarah and her health, you start to worry, and your mind jumps to the worst-case scenario: a life-threatening illness. (Turns out, there is none.) An intuitive thought happens in an instant, often in the form of an epiphany and with nothing attached to it. Even when it doesn't necessarily make sense or with no reasonable explanation, an intuitive thought carries the feeling of knowing. You find yourself thinking, *I don't know why, I just* know *it.* You call your friend Sarah and ask how she's feeling, and she tells you, "I was *just* about to call you. It's not life-threatening, but I need to have surgery."

Vocabulary Lesson

Mind Thoughts: Chatty, noisy, complicated, suspicious, exaggerated, defensive, judgmental, or critical thoughts that build upon one another.

Intuitive Thoughts: Concise, simple, definitive, direct, or neutral thoughts that pop into our awareness out of the blue. Unlike mind thoughts that come in the form of dialogue or narration, intuitive thoughts are less verbal. In other words, you don't hear them as much as you *feel* them.

Signs generally appear when we need them most. They're unexpected and right on time. Another true-life story: Chris and I recently received unexpected and unwanted news—the discovery of mold in our basement, which would likely mean moving the kids upstairs and a total renovation of the space. As I was mulling over the costs, the disruption, and the potential health threat, I dipped into fear. Into that dreaded feeling of, *what am I going to do?* And right on cue, my phone rang. It was my mom, calling to say that she didn't know why but that she was really feeling the need to check in. Talk about a mother's intuition. After I explained my situation, she said, "Becky, I'm here to help in any way I can. I just want you to know you're not alone." As I welled up with gratitude for Mom's sweet response to my unexpected dilemma, my cell phone turned on—out of the blue—and started playing "Unexpected" by Jonah Platt. I am not kidding, and that's not all. Within the hour, Katie, one of my oldest and best friends, reached out via text to tell me: BECKS, HAD A DISTURBING DREAM ABOUT YOU LAST NIGHT AND FELT YOUR UNSETTLED ENERGY. JUST WANTED YOU TO KNOW I'M THERE FOR YOU! Again, signs often come in threes, so I knew not to dismiss these moments as coincidence. I understood that I was receiving a clear message from my "ground crew," along with my Team Spirit in the same moment. Together, they were coming through to say—you are supported and surrounded in both the physical and spiritual realms. Together, *we've* got you. I took a deep breath and thanked them aloud for showing up and reminding me of this important truth. I AM supported. I AM surrounded.

Q: How do I know when I'm getting an intuitive hit versus when fear is talking?

A: It can be easy to mistake nervousness, anxiety, or fear as your intuition, so when in doubt, listen to your heart over your head. Again, the mind is deceptive. Tricky. It loves to create stories, exaggerate, fabricate, talk us into things or out of things we cannot see or explain. Our feelings don't lie, so if you're hit with clarity, inspiration, or an overwhelming feeling of being pulled away from or guided forward in one direction or another, your "team" is likely behind it. My friend Ashley describes her own struggle with fear this way:

"My continual struggle has been, when I think I've received a message, I question whether it is indeed a message from Spirit, or is it my fear-mind generating a scary potential outcome? I can recall three significant times in my life when I have foreseen an unwanted outcome but worried it was simply fear and not intuition. I ignored the guidance, and these outcomes did come to pass, leading me to believe that if you have a niggling feeling that starts as a whisper and then returns as a punch to the chest, listen. It may be more than fear; it may be insight. My approach now is to listen. To breathe into the fear and feel around for what's underneath it. Is it just fear or is there something more?"

I love what Ashley says about feeling *into and underneath* the fear because so many of us get stuck in analysis paralysis, when we become paralyzed by overthinking and overcontrolling. In the face of fear or uncertainty, the guidance I've received from Spirit is to stop pushing to make things happen or resisting to stop things from happening. Admit that you don't know the answer and ask your team to show you the next step forward. Humbly ask: Guide me. Help me through my fear. Show me the next right step so that I can feel safe moving forward.

When we release our grip on the outcome, and trust that the next right step will appear, it will. And when it does, take it, and thank your team for showing you the way. Allow yourself to be led forward on trust and faith that whatever happens is happening *for you.*

As you take guided actions, your expression of love and gratitude is the encouragement your Team Spirit desires. It motivates them to come through even stronger the next time because it signals to them that you are present, you're listening. By recognizing, acknowledging, and appreciating your team for reaching through time and space to support you will increase the frequency and consistency of the signs they send your way.

Putting Lessons to the Test

• • •

For Haven's sixth birthday, we splurged on a trip to Disneyland. I had my reservations. Historically, the "happiest place on Earth" proves challenging for me. Even when I set energetic boundaries, large crowds of people have a way of getting to me, or rather—on me. I liken myself to a sponge for other people's messy moods; I unintentionally sop them up. Still, I was ready to jump into the playground for Haven, my daughter who reminds me to relax and let loose, and have some fun, already. I was all in, but not without protection, of course. The morning of our adventure, I took a few extra minutes in the hotel bed to ground and center before heading into the frenetic energy of the theme park. Lying back on the hotel's oversize pillows, I visualized a swirl of gold and violet light activate my crown and flood downward and throughout my body. I set a heartfelt intention that should I bump into any low-energy vibes, they be neutralized and transmuted back into the higher frequency of light. I asked my team for a day of bliss, a *heavenly* day, as we made our way through the park.

Did they deliver? Even in an atmosphere ruled by external noise, my Team Spirit heard me and cut through the chaos with signs from the Other Side. It started when we slid into our rental car and Chris noticed that the mileage was 5,019. May 19— Haven's birthday! And it didn't stop there. With the assistance of a "lightning pass" that was a surprise gift from my mom, who joined us that day, we bypassed the long lines and were able to go on Haven's favorite ride, It's a Small World, more than once. After eight hours of attractions, soft-serve ice cream, funnel cakes, and clocking in at 20,000 steps, we arrived at a nearby restaurant to meet visiting family for dinner. As we pulled into a parking spot, I noticed the time: 5:19 p.m., a full-circle moment! Haven squealed with delight, and aside from my tired feet, my energy was still intact and able to meet the magical moment. I laughed at the synchronicity, too, and inwardly thanked my team for answering the call. As the four of us walked into the restaurant together, I sank into a feeling of deep gratitude for the signs that

I had received this day and receive every day. As if reading my thoughts, Haven, dressed in her Princess Belle gown, looked up at us and declared, "Best birthday ever." This kid proves time and time again that she is our Earth angel, here to remind us to trust in the unseen, to play and enjoy every day of this life, to believe in magic and to reach for Heaven on Earth.

Part III

Independent
Study Hall

CHAPTER 6

I AM Worthy

...

I met Beth soon after her father died of a heart attack at age seventy-seven. Prior to his abrupt departure from this world, he hadn't shown any signs or symptoms of ailing health. Beth came to me for a reading, hoping he'd come through. I shared with Beth what I tell all my clients who have special requests: you get who you need, and not always who you want. Meaning, *who* comes through is based on the emotional needs of the living and the dead, and that spirit delivers the messages considered to serve the "highest good" of the living recipients. I suggested to Beth that she try to surrender her expectations. Over the years I've discovered that Spirit's messages are a combination of both what's necessary for us to hear at a particular time as well as what we're *willing* to hear.

In Beth's case, it was her maternal grandmother, Ann, who reached across the divide and appeared as the very image of a classy woman. In my mind's eye, I saw this spirit dressed to the nines in a St. John knit suit with her hair and makeup perfectly done. This image was combined with a split-second flash of my deceased grandma Flo, who was a top salesperson at Saks Fifth Avenue in Los Angeles for over a decade. Her mantra: If you look good, you feel good. She believed that the beauty you wear on the outside should reflect the love you carry on the inside. When Grandma Flo appears in my readings, I recognize it as a sign that the spirit coming through embodied a similar philosophy.

Ann also wore a mask to accessorize her sharp appearance. This told me that she only *pretended* to embody a sense of self-worth and self-love throughout her lifetime. In an attempt to redeem this deceit, she stood next to Beth, acting in the role of her guide. I understood Ann's message to her granddaughter: heal the generational pattern of believing you're not enough. Through a series of images and impressions, Ann communicated that she'd passed this belief of low self-worth and false achievement onto her own daughter, Beth's still-living mother, who in turn, passed it down to Beth.

This generational struggle deeply resonated with Beth, who admitted that she'd felt the pressure to be "perfect" her whole life. "I come from a line of women who taught me to always strive to do and *be* more and . . . ," she emphasized, "to look the perfect part."

To that end, Beth shared that she'd married a successful talent agent and had spent most of their marriage trying to be enough for him, believing that her worth was defined by her outward appearance. She starved herself to become thin, and still, she said, "I never felt like I measured up to his expectations and I exhausted and abandoned myself in the process." Only recently, after the death of her father, had Beth determined it was time to bravely step out of the shadows of her husband and step forward just *as she is.* She asked for a divorce and returned to her own professional track as a screenwriter and producer.

"I'm working hard to break this pattern of perfectionism with myself and for my three girls," Beth said, "reminding them daily that they are enough, just as they are, and to stop being so hard on themselves."

"Your grandmother is nodding her head," I said, "confirming that this is one of your big life lessons—you're good enough, beautiful enough, smart enough, successful enough. You're also meant to be the teacher of this lesson for your mom, who is still deep in the struggle. Your grandmother is showing me an Energizer Bunny, which is my sign language for someone who keeps on going and going and never slows down or sits still. She's also making me feel like she's hard on herself, very self-critical and always striving for more, to do and be more, despite her own success. She needs your help with this lesson if she's ever going to *get it.*"

As soon as I said this, Beth's father-in-spirit stepped forward, indicating that he was also responsible for perpetuating this pattern. He did this by flashing an image of Adam Neumann from the Netflix documentary series *WeWork* in my head, my most recent binge-watching frame of reference, telling me that the spirit coming through was overly ambitious in life, defining his self-worth and overall success in life by his title and the quantity and quality of his material possessions.

"Your dad is showing me an image of driving through Manhattan throwing money up in the air," I said to Beth, "which tells me that when he was alive, he measured success in dollars, in 'net worth,' and now he's shaking his head with regret for putting possessions and his portfolio before everything else because he finally gets it—our lesson is to measure success in joy, the kind that comes from accepting who we are and believing in our own inherent worth. He is clapping his hands, applauding you for the work you're doing now in your lifetime to rewrite the family legacy, by breaking old patterns and embracing your worthiness."

"It's not easy," Beth admitted. "Old patterns are hard to break. It's far easier to slip back into doubt and insecurity, especially when I'm surrounded by people who are caught up in the material world and superficial measures of success. I feel like the black sheep in the family. What drives me forward is my girls and being an example for them. I *know* that they are enough"—she smiled with an undeniable mother's love—"and I want them to know it, too."

"Our world is filled with illusion and delusion," I said, "and it's easy to forget that people matter, not material things, titles, or portfolios. By showing your girls the contrast, a different way to feel and *be* in the world, you are healing your family—in the present, past, and future."

More Than Enough

• • •

I meet people like Beth every day who are struggling with beliefs about who they are, who they're "supposed" to be, what they deserve, and what they're capable of. Because these beliefs are often instilled in early childhood, and energetically passed down through family lines, we're not consciously aware of them. And yet, we *feel* them.

As you work to shift your beliefs around disconnection and separateness, remembering that you are connected and surrounded at every turn in your life, I want you also to keep in mind that *you* are enough. Just as you are. Can you feel into the space between feeling separate and alone and knowing that you are enough?

Take a moment now to bring your head and your heart into coherence by turning your thoughts down and your feelings up. As you get into heart/head alignment, take a look at the belief statements below.

Do any of them resonate with or sound familiar to you? Have you experienced or expressed these thoughts yourself, or has someone else expressed them to you?

I'm not _____ enough.

good

successful

attractive

smart fit

dependable

loveable

fun

wealthy

I don't deserve to be _____.

successful

happy financially secure

loved

healthy a parent

a boss/partner/manager/leader

It can feel painful to admit that we hold beliefs like these about ourselves. Remember that spirits describe this type of pain as Hell on Earth, where we become stuck in a spin cycle of hurt feelings and shadow beliefs, unconscious repetitive thoughts that, over time, we believe as truth. The work that you will do now is to unlearn these beliefs, and it starts with embracing one of the most important lessons of your lifetime:

Lesson 4: I AM Worthy.

I AM as worthy as anyone else.

I AM worthy. As I AM.

Every day, spirits come through in readings to remind the living that we are each worthy of abundance, compassion, respect, forgiveness, safety, protection, attention, good health, peace, and love. This message comes through loud and clear and still, in my professional experience, this lesson is the *one* that humans have the hardest time embracing. Often, in fact, clients will resist this lesson and yet it is so deserving of our attention because it affects all our relationships and how we feel, act, and react every day. In one of my favorite books, *Conversations with God: An Uncommon Dialogue*, author Neale Donald Walsch writes, "If you cannot love yourself, you cannot love another . . . You must first learn to honor and cherish and love your Self. You must first see your Self as worthy before you can see another as worthy. You must first see your Self as blessed before you can see another as blessed. You must first know your Self to be holy before you can acknowledge holiness in another."

Spirits echo Walsch's sentiments. Too often they express that one of their greatest regrets in life was not living in a way that was aligned with who they really are, mainly because they fell under the spell of feeling unworthy. They bought into a story, a false narrative that affects so many aspects of our lives—how intimate we can be with others, how effective we can be at work, how courageous we can be at trying new things and taking risks, how happy and free we can feel in our lives. And from what I've observed, this "spell" tends to be passed down from one generation to the next. In readings, spirits come through to apologize to their still-living loved ones for unconsciously shaming, blaming, editing, and controlling their actions and reactions, and ultimately inhibiting their independence and growth. Once on the Other Side, some of these same spirits recognize how they projected their own lack of self-worth onto those around them, in particular their children, and they finally understand this simple truth: we cannot give to others what we don't have within ourselves. When we unintentionally step on another person's worth, it is because we struggle with our own worth. When we withhold love from others, it is because we withhold love and regard for ourselves. During the life review process, spirits are shown a mirror to see what they reflected outwardly to the world. Those who had a limited view of themselves had lives marked by limitation, and they come forward with urgency, encouraging their living loved ones to unsubscribe from this false narrative.

Changing this narrative has been lifelong work for me, and I resonate with this lesson deeply. In chapter one, I shared my journey of tracing my lifelong struggle with money back to a childhood belief that "I am not enough." Projected onto me by my dad, I believed that my worth was directly proportional to putting other people's needs before my own, so I was convinced that *I'm not okay if you're not okay.* Combined with my high sensitivity and empathic nature, I learned how to self-abandon and self-forget and negate my own needs in an effort to be the "easy" kid who maintains the household peace. I played the role of listener and therapist for my dad and the babysitter for my little brother as an unconscious need to feel needed. As an adult, I measured my worth in dollars, buying people's respect, acceptance, devotion, and love, believing again, that if they needed me, they wouldn't abandon me. I finally realized that this belief was bankrupting me—financially, emotionally, and spiritually. Gaining this self-awareness more than a decade ago changed my life. However, it wasn't until a recent session with Jakki that I finally gained clarity around what this struggle was intended to teach me. When she was running my energy with the color of royal blue, my Team Spirit came through loud and clear with the following message: I don't have to give anything away to receive love and devotion. My worth is not tied to what I can *do*; my worth is tied to who I AM. I AM worthy of love. I AM worthy. Just as I AM.

Recognize the Pattern

• • •

You, or someone you know, may have grown up similarly, with a parent or a caregiver whose wounds resulted from intergenerational patterns of false beliefs. If you were raised by parents who struggled with their self-worth, they were probably incapable of instilling confidence in you. This isn't about assigning blame or fault; we're all here in Earth School together. Let's assume your parents and caregivers did the best they could, given their level of self-awareness and the tools they had at their disposal. And let's hope our kids and grandkids (if we have them) afford us the same compassion and understanding.

Over the years, I've noticed how my own struggle has shown up in my sons. My older son, Jakob, has a habit of spending money he doesn't have and going into debt as a result, and his younger brother, Sam, has picked up my pattern of spending his savings to buy his friends' snacks and other things simply as a means to buy their friendship and devotion. I acknowledge my role in their false belief system, that how I feel or have felt about my worth affects their sense of worthiness. To own my part, I sat down with them recently and shared my struggle. I said something like, "Even though I'm your mom, I'm growing up alongside you guys and when I first became a parent, I didn't have the self-worth that I have now and because of that I sometimes made choices and did things that weren't helpful to you."

"Like what?" Sam jumped in, always eager for specifics.

"For instance, I may have said or done things, unintentionally, that made you feel unseen or unheard, diminished, deflated, not good enough, less than. And for any and all of that, I am sorry. You are worthy, valuable, and loved just as you are. Just for being born."

"Thanks, Mom," Sam said while making a move to get up off the couch, his signal that our cozy family meeting was "over."

"It's okay, Mom," added Jakob as he, too, stood up. "You do your best, even though it's not perfect."

I can live with imperfect, I thought to myself as they walked into the kitchen and threw open the fridge, pulling out half of the contents until they decided to fight over who got to eat the last slice of pizza.

"It's mine," Sam insisted.

"Give it to me," Jakob ordered.

I smiled and thought, *They seem to be learning to stand up for their worth after all.*

Set a New Pattern in Motion

• • •

False narratives are often just thoughts that you've repeated to yourself over time, or that you've adopted from a parent, caregiver, teacher, or from someone who played a significant role in your life. But repetition and projection don't make these beliefs true. You likely created and repeated these beliefs about yourself to protect yourself, to survive an event, a specific period of your life, or a relationship. While these beliefs may have worked for you at a certain time, they tend to become outdated and can work against you until you change the narrative:

I am underserving. I am not enough. ⮑

I AM worthy of a full life.

Reassess Your Worth

· · ·

When you change outdated, false beliefs about yourself and recognize that you are worthy of so much more than you've afforded yourself, the qualities you believed you lacked or had a deficit begin to expand, and this is what your soul has been waiting for and nudging you to remember—that you are enough just as you are.

I recognized Karmen, the owner of A Line Boutiques in Denver, as soon as she entered my group session. I knew she was a successful businesswoman, but I didn't know much about her personal life. As she took a seat on my office couch, I became curious what messages Spirit would have for her.

Once I began the reading and I moved my focus around the room, I felt the presence of masculine energy hovering around Karmen. I intuitively felt that the spirit coming forward was that of her father as he put his hands on her shoulders, my sign for support. He also bowed his head while patting her on the back, which I interpreted as a combination of regret and pride. I said to Karmen, "I believe your dad is here and he's sorry for not saying this enough when he was alive: he's very proud of you."

Karmen heard me but remained neutral in her response. I sensed that she was holding on to some resentment toward her father and that his words from beyond weren't penetrating.

"Your mother is also here," I said, pivoting away from Karmen's dad, "and she's showing me an olive branch, my sign for forgiveness. She's standing with your dad, which tells me that they are united on the Other Side."

Karmen nodded with tears in her eyes, fully engaged now as she heard this message from her mother.

"She's also showing me a white dog who has been by your side, teaching you how to receive unconditional love."

"That's my dog Bagley," Karmen acknowledged.

"He's part of your ground crew, here to help you open your heart."

The spirit of Karmen's mother faded as quickly as she entered, and sensing that Karmen wasn't receptive to her father's presence, I moved on to read others in the group.

Nearly a full year after her reading, I ran into Karmen in one of her clothing boutiques, and after chatting for a minute or two about fashion, she shared: "When I saw you for the reading, I wasn't interested in hearing from my dad. Actually, I doubted that he would come through. He abandoned me in life, and I doubted he would behave any differently in death. I'd hoped that my mom would have a message for me, and I was grateful she did. After the reading, though, I sat with my dad's message, and I softened a bit. If what he said is true—that he is sorry—I'm open to hearing that."

I felt an intuitive nudge and I offered, "Hey, would you be interested in being included in my current book project?"

"I'd love to," Karmen agreed and surprised me by saying, "plus it only seems fair, since I wrote you into mine." *Say what?* She ducked into the back room and emerged with a book titled *Learning to Fly*. I held her book in my hands and felt clearly that our paths had meant to cross. Thanks, guides, I thought to myself.

Later that evening, I poured through Karmen's book, becoming even more curious about her relationship with her father and her childhood longing to capture his attention. When she agreed to meet me a few days later, I launched right in: "Can you tell me more about the struggle with your dad? It deeply resonates with me."

"Dad was all about making millions of dollars, so overly ambitious," she began. "The message I received was that success and money were everything to him, and as a result, he was in and out of my life pursuing the next best deal. My parents divorced when I was five, and Dad would be gone for long stretches of time, and he never apologized or even acknowledged his absence when he returned. Again, his focus was always on his latest deal, which was of no importance to me. I just wanted my dad.

"I concluded that to be loved by my dad, I had to be more like him—above average, competitive, number one in my class. I had to prove my worth, and I never measured up. He wasn't there for me, while my mom always showed up for me and my sister until she passed away from a brain tumor when I was seventeen."

"I'm so sorry," I said as I felt Karmen's loss. Has anything shifted for you since the reading?"

"I started talking to Dad after the reading. On a solo trip to the mountains, I welcomed his presence and asked him: 'Why did you choose money over me?' I visualized his face, and I believe he answered me."

"And?" I asked with anticipation.

"His message was that he thought he was going to make us money and then have all the time in the world with me and my sister, but then one week turned into a month which turned into a year which turned into a decade, which turned into his life."

I shared with Karmen that many spirits come through with messages of clarity and regret like this one. They hadn't meant to squander their time here, to miss their kids' childhood, to miss out on important relationships, to focus on work and achieving above everything else.

"I finally understood him as I was writing about him," Karmen said. "When my dad behaved as if I needed to be perfect to be worthy of his love, it was coming from his own deep wounds—he believed that he wasn't 'good enough' unless he was perfect, and he projected that drive for perfection onto me. It finally made sense in a twisted kind of way, and understanding that has allowed me to forgive him and start to heal."

"You're healing yourself *and* you're helping your dad heal on the Other Side," I said. "And, you're modeling a different kind of self-worth for your daughter."

"That's the goal," Karmen said. "This pattern stops with me. My hope for my daughter is that she will never solely attach her worth to accomplishments or achievements. Every night I whisper in her ear: 'You're enough. You're beautiful, you're whole. You're worthy.'"

Exercise

. . . .

Wash Yourself with Royal Blue

To feel your way back to the fundamental truth that you are worthy, you will "run the color" of royal blue and rose gold throughout your body to align with the energy of worthiness and gratitude.

Close your eyes and take several deep breaths to ground you in the present moment. Sit up straight with your feet on the ground and your hands resting in your lap. Pull your shoulder blades back and drop them down, and feel your chest push out and forward. Now, center your focus on the crown of your head and visualize royal blue light flooding down like a waterfall or a cup overflowing, descending down your spinal column, all the way to the soles of your feet. The energetic frequency of blue light works to deprogram your mind and body of old patterns, false beliefs, and fear-based, limited thinking. Visualize this blue light circulating in an infinity flow throughout your entire being, from head to toe, and back up again. Feel this energy flow up and down your chakra system, cleansing your physical, mental, emotional, and etheric bodies. (Again, if visualization is a challenge for you, use your physical senses. As an example, take a shower and imagine that you are standing underneath a bright blue waterfall. Or meditate before a body of water or a fountain.)

Next, I want you to infuse that blue waterfall with flecks of rose gold and visualize it circulating throughout your entire body and pooling in your heart. Imagine the light of rose gold expanding your heart chakra and aligning you with the frequency of worthiness and gratitude for your perfectly imperfect self. Take a deep breath. Can you feel gratitude for all that you are, just as you are? Can you feel gratitude for simply being alive?

As you continue the visualization of rose gold pumping throughout your heart, tap at least three times on the "karate chop" point from the diagram on page 78. As you tap, repeat any or all of the following set-up statements. Choose the sentiments that most resonate with you or feel free to make up your own, either repeating the same or different statements each time.

- Even though I have created false stories about myself . . . I AM opening to the truth.
- Even though I feel like I am always messing up or that I have failed . . . I AM worthy of forgiveness. I AM worthy of respect.
- Even though I am struggling, in suffering, in pain . . . I AM worthy of peace. I AM worthy of happiness.
- Even though I feel scared and uncertain . . . I AM worthy of security.
- Even though I think that I don't fit in . . . I AM worthy of love and acceptance.
- Even though I feel shame about my body . . . I AM worthy of compassion.
- Even though I feel invisible or invaluable . . . I AM worthy of being seen and heard.
- Even though I have lost faith and trust in myself . . . My soul knows that I AM worthy.

After tapping on the "karate chop" point, follow with a round of *feeling* statements that affirm the truth of how you feel. As you tap on the remaining eight meridian points—starting at the eyebrow point and ending at the top of your head—express an emotion, along with any other thoughts that come up for you. This could be a single word or just a sound.

Follow this round with another full round of tapping on all eight meridian points, while repeating the following I AM statements again:

- I AM opening to the truth.
- I AM worthy of forgiveness. I AM worthy of respect.
- I AM worthy of peace. I AM worthy of happiness.
- I AM worthy of security.
- I AM worthy of love and acceptance.
- I AM worthy of compassion.
- I AM worthy of being seen and heard.
- My soul knows that I AM worthy.

As you tap and repeat the I AM statements, ask your Team Spirit to help you shift and uplift your energy out of illusion and delusion, out of the shadows and into the higher vibrational frequencies of light and unconditional love and acceptance.

Continue to breathe IN: I AM. Breathe OUT: WORTHY.

Q: Rebecca, self-worth is an important lesson for me, but the words *selfish* and *self-important* carry so much negative weight, at least in my family, where it was frowned upon. Can you distinguish between the two?

A: Growing self-worth or worthiness is not the same as an inflated sense of self. Being self-*centered* or self-*serving*, where you feel entitled to, better than, more important, powerful, or more special than another, is low-energy stuff. And false. No one is better than another. Having a strong and healthy self-worth, on the other hand, is high-energy stuff. Worthiness grounds us into our bodies and allows us to embrace our individuality and uniqueness. Worthiness cultivates self-love where we recognize we are worthy simply because we exist, and that we are perfectly imperfect one-of-a-kind expressions of Spirit. The goal is to dial into a healthy state of worthiness where we humbly receive and gracefully accept richness in all its many forms—in love, in friendships, in security and comfort.

One of the many things that Spirit has shared with me is that when we are born, we come into this world in our purest state, our souls having recently been immersed in the light, love, and oneness of the spirit world. Our self-worth is completely intact, but as we are conditioned into this Earthly realm, if we don't hold tight to this sense of love and worth, it can easily become buried or depleted. We choose our parents, our family dynamics, and every other detail of our earthly life to give us the best opportunities to *relearn* this lesson.

Over the years, my Team Spirit has encouraged me to inherit my birthright and to just be me despite what others think. Early on in my mediumship practice, this was a tall order. I wanted so badly to be normal. To have normal gifts. A normal job. A normal life. I finally realized that there is no such thing as "normal" and more important, shrinking down and dimming my light to fit into someone else's idea of normal dishonors my inherent worth. As the late Wayne Dyer said, "What you think about me is none of my business."

What does matter, what is my business, is what *I* think about myself. What do you think about yourself?

Worthy of Love

• • •

On a phone reading, the strong energy of a female spirit came through, flashing an image of my own maternal figures into my mind. This told me that I was feeling a maternal presence, and I could sense this female energy to the right of my client, a woman named Connie. This spirit showed me her hands pressed together with her head bowed, my sign for gratitude and being thankful. She also flashed in my mind a mental picture of me and Haven, further indication that Connie was this spirit's daughter.

I said to Connie, "I'm seeing a mother spirit with you. Did your mother pass away? She's showing me an image of you standing next to her bed, holding her hand. Did you take care of her at the end of her life?"

"Yes!" Connie exclaimed. "I was with her in the hospital when she passed and had been her primary caretaker for the past couple of years, as she was needing more help getting around and taking care of herself and the house."

"She's showing me a cloud of pink light in the room and all around her, to say that she could feel your love up until the very end, and she wants you to know that your devotion and care helped her make the transition from this life to the next with ease. She wants you to know that she was at peace when she passed in her sleep, and now she wants to bless your life by sending you a new partner in love. She's showing me two gold bands linked together, my sign for romantic love, and she's impressing me with the feelings of butterflies in my stomach, like having a sense of eager anticipation or being excited to see someone."

Connie smiled with some hesitation. "I got divorced two years ago and felt really isolated and alone during the height of the pandemic. It would be nice to meet someone," she admitted.

"Your mom is doing what she can on the Other Side to inspire a new relationship and manifest miracles in your life, and she's rolling up her sleeves, meaning that you must do your part, too. Your work is to open your heart so that you can be open to the level of love and attention that you are capable of receiving. I'm seeing a metal chest piece like armor over your heart, as if you have energetically built up 'a wall' around your heart since your divorce. Until you lower your wall, you will remain closed off from new love and new relationships. Does that make sense?"

Connie nodded her head and added, "It was easy to love Mom, especially at the end, when all I had left was love for her. But when it comes to other people, it's harder for me. It's true that I put up a wall. I guess it's a trust issue."

"Your mom is showing me that she struggled in this way, too. Did she also divorce?"

Connie nodded. "She and my dad split when I was young and she remarried twice, and those marriages ended, too."

"Your mom struggled with her worthiness. She didn't trust that she was loveable, or ultimately worthy of love. She's showing me a generational pattern here of not feeling enough. And while we do not need anyone else to feel complete, whole, or to be loved, we do learn an important lesson about our own worth through our relationships with others. Mom is shaking her head with regret, to say that she failed to learn this lesson—that we are *all* worthy of love, just as we are. It's now your work to change this old pattern of putting up a wall and pushing love away. By welcoming a new relationship, you 'break the chain,' you neutralize an old belief that's false. By believing in your own worthiness—that you deserve and are entitled to love—and by allowing yourself to receive love from others, you will help to release some of your mom's distrust and fear of abandonment and rejection. As you open to love, so will she."

Connie took a deep breath. "This feels like *a lot.*"

I paused, inwardly reminding myself to slow down. Healing old wounds, past, present, and future can feel overwhelming. It's big and beautiful stuff, and I sometimes forget how *big* it is because I work in the unseen world of the weird every day.

"It's a lot of information at once," I acknowledged. "But when you make up your mind to open your heart, if only a little bit at a time, you will start to heal your family pattern. It starts with intention. Set the intention to open and receive, and as you do—know that you are worthy. You are worthy of love."

Grow the Feeling through Inspired Action

• • •

The energetic vibration of worthiness *feels* like love, and by raising your energy through visualizations and repetitive practices like tapping, you will experience a shift. Still, to truly grow and embody a new feeling, one that brings you closer to heaven, you must also actively live your life in alignment with that feeling. That said, putting the lesson that I AM worthy into practice can be challenging because even if you believe and know it to be true, that's only half of the assignment. The second part, *feeling and embodying* it, is harder to achieve.

In my own life, Spirit continues to test my feelings of worthiness by presenting me with new situations that test my learning. For example, I have become mindful to gratefully accept money when it is rightfully mine, and to have and hold on to it before I unconsciously give it away. As a regular practice, when I write out and sign checks to employees, pay online bills, or hand the cashier my credit card, I mentally thank Spirit for providing to me what I need while mentally affirming: I AM worthy of having my needs met. I AM worthy of security. While this practice may sound silly, I've learned that changing old beliefs, and old patterns of behavior, doesn't just happen overnight. I wish it did! Instead, it requires intention and dedicated attention and for me and my money struggle, I've noticed that my intentional "bill-pay" practice settles my nervous system and helps me to feel safe in uncertain and insecure times.

How will *you* grow the feeling of worthiness through inspired action? One idea is to focus on a person, an organization, an idea, or a cause you deeply believe in. What feelings come up? Love? Compassion? Admiration? Respect? Pride? Whatever the feeling, magnify that feeling in your heart. Really let it swell and then offer it to yourself. Breathe it in. Allow worthiness to open and expand your heart to receive the love, respect, admiration, and compassion that is your birthright.

CHAPTER 7

I AM Here to Heal
+ Contribute

. . .

I met Andrea when she came to see me for a one-on-one reading. She was reeling from grief after a string of consecutive losses within a single year that most of us could not fathom enduring within an entire lifetime: the loss of her mother to a neurological disease, the loss of her father to suicide, and the loss of her husband to a prescription drug overdose.

Almost as soon as I opened up the channel between this world and the next, I could feel a strong male energy rushing forward, eager to be first in line. This spirit's energy was desperate, a combination of love and regret at the same time. My intuition told me that it was her husband.

"I feel the spirit of your husband is here, and I can also feel his urgent desire to lift heavy guilt and grief off you. He's also showing me an image of Dr. Jekyll and Mr. Hyde. Did he have a conflicted personality?" I asked.

Andrea nodded sadly. "From the day we were married, Paul was an amazing partner. He was fun and generous. He was driven and successful, and I had no doubt he loved me dearly. On the flip side, however, his moods could dramatically shift. As the 'peacemaker' type this was terribly distressing to me, and whenever I'd try to talk to him about it, he refused to acknowledge that it was a problem he should change or deal with."

"He's also showing me an AA coin, my sign for substance abuse and that this pattern went on for many years of your marriage," I suggested.

"For twenty years or so," Andrea confirmed. "As the years ticked on, I was increasingly unhappy in our marriage. We spoke of divorce but slogged our way through. I probably should have spoken up louder and left before we had kids, but I stayed the course and was silently resentful."

"I am literally feeling your anger and resentment in my throat."

"Oh my gosh," Andrea said as she put her hands to her throat. "In 2015, I developed vocal problems that my doctor said could be safely treated with surgery, but I did not recover fully. I couldn't speak at all for a full six weeks, and I am still not one hundred percent recovered. This was devastating for me, as I have been a singer my whole life and the thought of never being able to sing again threw me into a deep depression."

As she said "depression," I felt mother energy step forward. "I think your mother is here. She's placing a hand on the top of your head, extending gratitude for caring for her at the end of her life. Does this ring true?"

Andrea welled up. "A few years ago, Mom was diagnosed with some neurological condition akin to ALS, and I did a lot of caregiving for her in the end. It was painful and slow, and even though we were relieved that she was finally free of her body, it was devastating. My father just couldn't recover, and two months after she passed, he took his life. At the same time, Paul had relapsed again, and it was all that I could take. After losing both my parents and suffering in a lonely marriage for twenty years, I decided to stop lying to myself, to stop holding back the tears and holding in the screams. No more, I told myself. Enough is enough." Andrea took a deep breath as the tears fell. "And then, five days after I asked for a divorce, Paul took his life, too."

I could feel the immense weight of Andrea's heavy heart along with a sinking pit in my stomach. Deep grief. I reached out and squeezed her hand. "He's saying that it was not your fault or the result of you asking for a divorce, and he is so sorry to you and the kids for doing what he did. He's showing me trauma that goes back four generations that he failed to address in his lifetime."

I shared with Andrea that I could clairvoyantly "see" a little boy in a fetal position with ghostly shadows lined up along his left side, my sign that the trauma was carried through the paternal line.

"Paul now understands that addressing this generational trauma was his work to do, and even though you were his 'rock,' it was not yours to take on. Your work isn't to save anyone—your mom, your dad, your husband. Your dad is jumping in on this message, too. Caring for your mom took an immense toll on him, and he forgot himself in the process. He doesn't want you to repeat this pattern. Your guides are showing me your hands extended outward, meaning that you are really good at putting everyone else's needs first, but your work is to tend to yourself, to care for and love yourself. Spirit is showing me a 'radio channel,' as if to say that you must tune in to your inner voice. Use it to speak up for yourself and honor what's true for *you*. In time, this is how you will heal and how you will model healing for your kids and others."

A few months after the reading, I received this hopeful email from Andrea:

> I am currently under the care of a vocal coach who is work-
> ing with the muscular tension in my throat, the result of over
> several decades of extreme stress and trauma. In addition,
> I'm getting regular massages that directly address my throat
> chakra to help it to open and relax. In the fall, I will return to
> my job as a therapeutic musician playing and singing at the
> bedside of patients and helping them feel more whole, more
> relaxed and connected to Spirit regardless of their medical
> status. It is healing work for both the patients and for me, and
> I am grateful to do it and humbly be the conduit.

What's Your Hidden Strength?

• • •

As Andrea's story beautifully illustrates, once we bravely begin the process of healing ourselves, we can step into our authenticity and fulfill our life's work. Spirits routinely encourage the living to confront our biggest struggles—fear of failure, alienation, heartbreak, inadequacy, or loss. Fear of speaking up and asking for what we need. Fear of stepping forward to be seen. Whatever hard feelings that we wrestle with the most, spirits share that they have shown up in our lives as an opportunity to help us heal our past, present, and future. That's the big secret. Within our deepest struggle is our greatest opportunity. Even further—within our deepest struggle is our greatest *strength*. Imagine that? The thing you've always thought was in your way and holding you back was designed (by you!) to propel you forward. The question is: Will you harness the strength hidden within your struggle?

When I posed this question to Andrea, she offered, "I still feel shipwrecked over all that I've lost, but I understand now that everything that has happened was meant to be. My dear and broken husband ultimately taught me to love myself, to become the strong woman I am today, and to model a healthy path forward for both my daughter and my son, and for those to come after them."

In my line of work, I meet inspiring people every day who remind me how to live, and Andrea's story is a perfect example of what it means to tackle **Lesson 5: I AM here to heal. I AM here to contribute.**

Once you embrace the truth that you are worthy you can step into your strength, your power and purpose, the "what" you're here to do in this life. In *Awaken the Spirit Within*, I shared what Spirit has communicated to me—that each of us is born with the same purpose—to embody, express, and extend the highest frequencies of love and light to the world around us. This is our life's "work," and while we each have a similar job to do, the specifics of what we do and how we do it vary based on our individual strengths, interests, and talents. For some, our best expression may be through art, while others gravitate toward teaching, or science, or business. We each approach our life's work uniquely, and what I've observed is that those who have channeled their struggle into a strength, one that allows them to heal and contribute to the healing of others, are the happiest and most fulfilled. As examples, Jenny, who always struggled with her body

image, became a model and advocate for body positivity and in-
clusiveness, eventually creating a fashion line that celebrates all
body types. Dylan, who grew up in poverty and wrestled with a
lifelong fear of "losing it all" started an organization that funds
affordable housing in gentrified areas. Corey, who has five siblings and, as a child, always struggled to feel seen and heard, became a high school drama teacher who encourages his students
to use their voices and step into the spotlight. Lisa, who lived
with an abusive husband for two decades, found the courage to
leave her marriage and get help, and years later became a counselor volunteering at a shelter for battered women. All of these
people found a way to confront their struggles and connect to a
sense of purpose that not only helped them heal, but also helped
others to heal, and by embracing a calling motivated by their
drive to heal and contribute, they each live in a higher energetic
state, radiating all of the beautiful qualities that humans can pos-
sess. This is the work we are here to do.

Contract, Work, and Purpose: What's the Difference?

People often ask me: What's the difference between our "contract" and life's "work" or "purpose"? Or are they the same
thing? This is a great question, and one I'm excited to answer.
Here's what I've learned from Spirit: every one of us comes into
this world with a "prebirth contract" that loosely outlines the
lessons we're meant to learn and to teach others in this lifetime,
along with the opportunities and experiences that will allow us
to best succeed in these endeavors and spiritually advance. Once

we're here, we create "postbirth contracts" or "agreements" that may or may not conflict with our prebirth contract. For example, if one of your primary prebirth lessons is to learn how to forgive and heal in this lifetime and instead, you've gotten caught in a spin cycle of resentment and blame, or you've made agreements with false beliefs that are not your own (typically through childhood programming or cultural conditioning), then your prebirth and postbirth contracts are working against each other. Spirit has shared that much of our "work" is to become conscious of this conflict or misalignment. Once we remember, and then reconcile and honor, our prebirth contracts, we can fulfill our "soul purpose."

We each have a soul purpose that was scripted before we were born, and the clue to what yours is *lies within your struggle*. Struggling with feelings of irrelevancy and invisibility, for example, can be channeled into a strength, one from which you build your life's work, such as helping others to find the courage to step forward and feel seen. This work, specific to you, infuses your life with meaning and purpose. You follow? The diamond in the rough—the strength within your struggle—isn't necessarily obvious or easy to find, but there's one in there somewhere and it wants to be discovered. I recently worked with a man named Matt who suffered verbal abuse as a child and as an adult, he struggled to assert his own voice. Despite his challenge, he eventually became a community organizer for at-risk kids, like he once was, in need of representation and advocacy. Matt channeled his childhood struggle into purposeful work. He found his diamond. And if he hadn't discovered his own brilliant gem? Failing to learn an important lesson like "I AM worthy of being seen and heard" could have prevented him from growing into the man he was meant to be, one who helps others discover their own diamond in the rough. What a loss that would have been.

To be clear—Matt's "purpose" isn't to be a community organizer. We aren't our work. The mind loves to confuse identity, the *who* we are with *what* we do. Admittedly, this can be a head scratcher, so it's important to separate the two. Take what I do, for example. I'm a spiritual medium. Being able to talk to the dead is my unique craft, and it's the nine-to-five job that I do. My true life's work, however, is to learn my key lessons and to help others learn theirs. Spirit assures me that in the grand scheme of things, title, position, professional ranking, and power mean nothing. It doesn't matter *what* you do. Your "Earth job" is a means to an end—it is the vessel through which you fulfill your spiritual assignments.

We're each drawn to different paths and professions, none better or worse, or more or less important than another, based on our individual gifts, skills, and preferences and where we can make the most healing impact. I've met nurses, doctors, school counselors, therapists, bodyworkers, childcare workers, attorneys, manicurists, real estate agents, bank tellers, parole officers, mail carriers, and stay-at-home parents who have used their "work" in very different ways to complete their own assignments and also elevate others. Again, it's not what you *do*. Spirit tells me that it's the *intention* behind what you do that matters most. Giving back to your community for "likes" on social media, for example, is not the same thing as being generous because your heart drives you to give. True generosity doesn't need recognition, a pat on the back. True generosity does not give to get. Spirits relay that when our actions, reactions, responses, words, and deeds are authentic, loving, and kind, we're living our life on purpose. When we show up, day to day, with a sincere intention to honor ourselves and have a positive impact on the people and the world around us, we're doing our best work.

Change the Narrative

• • •

Healing is particularly hard work, and sometimes it's challenging to believe that what we're doing matters or has a purpose. What Spirit has shown me is that when we choose to channel our struggle into an opportunity to heal ourselves and others, we begin to understand our purpose, what we're here to contribute to the world. If you're feeling uncertain about the role you're playing in your own life, it's time to change the false narrative that may be preventing you from stepping forward:

I am broken. I am irrelevant. My "work" lacks meaning. ⇨

I AM here to heal. I AM here to contribute. I AM here on purpose.

My client Dirck received this message directly from his deceased mother when he attended one of my large audience readings. She appeared as a bright orb to his right side and clairvoyantly showed me two open books side by side, my sign that her death and his life were linked and that he had work to do to heal a generational pattern of dysfunction and a false belief that he was broken.

"Your mother is handing you an olive branch," I said, "which means she wants you to forgive something or someone. I'm also seeing 'AA,' my sign for addiction. Does this make sense to you?"

"It does. Alcohol runs very deep on both sides of my family," Dirck said.

"I'm seeing a long line of people, my sign that it travels back many generations."

"My grandfather was a white lightning moonshine maker," Dirck confirmed, "and from my earliest memories, alcohol was abused by all my family members. As a kid, I didn't know any different because that was the environment I grew up in and it was a part of our family identity. It became part of my identity, too. I was a binge-drinking alcoholic for twenty-two years. I'm sober now."

"Your mother is flashing me a peace sign, as if to say that you're being called to forgive the generations that came before you who led you down the same path. They were living in their own fear, coping in their own way, and surviving the best they knew how. But you're meant to do more than survive. Your mom is showing me two girls. Do you have daughters?" I asked.

"Yes." Dirck nodded. "Two daughters and one son."

"By consciously choosing differently, you break a cycle of destructive behavior in your family line that will allow your own children to grow up differently. By healing yourself, you set a new pattern in motion."

A year after his reading, I received the following email:

It's been one year exactly to the day that you gave me a reading that changed the trajectory of my path here on Earth, and for the generations that follow me. Your guidance reignited my hope and allowed me to redirect my life. I feel like I am now living my "purpose" and learning the true reasons I was put here to learn: to lead by example and be that role model I never had for my own kids. I've since started my own business of healing. I became a Reiki Master, and with my business partner, we started a small men's group for spiritual and personal growth to help men along their Earthly journey. I am forever grateful.

Exercise

• • • •

Wash Yourself with Emerald Green

In addition to repeating the I AM mantra to align with the truth that you are here to heal and contribute to the world in your own special way, you will "run the color of emerald green" throughout your body to push out fear, illusion, and confusion and raise your energy to align with Spirit. I've specifically chosen emerald green for this exercise because green is often interpreted as the color of authentic creative abundance from a Divine source. Emerald green vibrates at the level of consciousness equivalent to courage, neutrality, and willingness, which is incompatible with the low vibration of purposelessness and apathy. You will run emerald green through your system to release this shadow energy and spark the energy of new beginnings, healing, and spiritual growth.

Close your eyes and take several deep breaths to ground you in the present moment. Sit up straight with your feet on the ground and your hands resting in your lap. Pull your shoulder blades back and drop them down and push your heart forward. With each breath, focus on relaxing your entire body, from the top of your head down through your feet. Once you feel centered and grounded, imagine a beam of light extending up and through your crown, moving past this dimension, into the higher frequencies of the heavenly realm and connecting you to Spirit.

Next, focus on your feet and envision another beam of light extending from the sole of each foot that travels deep down into Earth's soil, and farther down into the core of Earth.

Once you feel connected above and below, move your attention to your heart center. Visualize a spark of emerald-green light begin to glow there. Continue to breathe. With each inhalation, visualize this emerald-green light pumping your strong and steady heart. As it grows more and more intense, visualize the light expanding, loosening, opening, and unblocking your heart, allowing for healing to freely flow. Breathe deeply and easily. (Remember, if visualization is a challenge for you, use your physical senses. Can you get outside in nature? Sit under a tree or on a patch of grass where you focus on the greenery surrounding you? If you are not accessible to the outdoors, can you settle your eyes on an office or house plant, or deliberately meditate on a green stone or a piece of emerald jewelry that you place in your hand?) Once you have a mental picture or a visual representation of emerald-green light running through you, tap at least three times on the karate chop point from the diagram on page 78. As you tap, repeat any or all of the following set-up statements that particularly resonate with you.

- Even though I feel battered and broken by life . . . I AM open to healing.
- Even though I feel aimless and lost . . . I trust that I AM here on purpose.

- Even though I am suffering and in pain . . . I AM willing to see the opportunity in my struggle.
- Even though I feel unclear . . . I AM stronger than I know.
- Even though I have forgotten my purpose . . . I AM here to contribute to the healing of others.
- Even though I feel invisible . . . I AM a bright shining star and the lead actor in my life.

After tapping on the "karate chop" point, follow with a round or two of *feeling* statements that affirm the truth of how you feel. As you tap on the remaining eight meridian points—starting at the eyebrow point and ending at the top of the head—express an emotion that you're struggling with, along with any other thoughts that come up for you. It could be a single word . . . "invisible," "unclear," "aimless" . . . or even a single sound . . . "yuck" or simply, "I hate this feeling."

Next, follow with another full round of tapping on all eight meridian points, while repeating the I AM statements again:

- I AM open to healing.
- I trust that I AM here on purpose.
- I AM willing to see the opportunity in my struggle.
- I AM stronger than I know.
- I AM here to contribute to the healing of others.
- I AM a bright shining star and the lead actor in my life.

As you tap through the meridian points while repeating the I AM statements, ask your Team Spirit to help you shift and uplift your energy out of illusion and delusion, out of the shadows and into the higher vibrational frequencies of neutrality, acceptance, and trust.

Continue to breathe IN: I AM. Breathe OUT: here to heal and contribute. I belong.

Healing to Change Our Patterns

• • •

To heal ourselves and others, we must not only change our beliefs and elevate our energy—we must also put our intentions into action by changing default behavior patterns. An opportunity to do this came up recently in my own family.

It was the week leading up to Mother's Day, and as the weekend approached, I noticed a significant shift in Chris's energy and mood. Over the past ten years of living with my husband, I've noticed that big holidays can be emotionally charged for him. I know the family history: Chris doesn't feel like his family shows up for him, even though he shows up for all of them. Since he was a kid, he's felt on the outside, unseen and unworthy of his family's attention and love, and these unhealed childhood wounds can set off a major funk.

On Sunday, my mother, along with my two brothers, my sister-in-law, and my nieces and nephews, came over to our house for a barbecue. Chris had extended the invitation to his mom, too, and halfway through the afternoon, I intuitively knew that she wasn't coming and that the bouquet of spring flowers he'd bought for her would not be hand delivered. Later that afternoon, after everyone left, I sat down with Chris, and he finally gave way to tears.

"I always try to bring my family together for holidays and I'm always disappointed. I don't know why I keep trying. . . ." he trailed off.

I held his hand and listened. He continued, "It's really hard to see how your family shows up for you, and for all of us. The contrast between your family and mine is painful, and I feel myself start to become resentful and I don't like that either." He turned to me. "I'm really struggling with this pattern, babe. It doesn't change and it makes me so sad, over and over again."

I looked deep into his eyes. "I feel how painful it is for you and unfortunately. . . ." I paused before saying what I knew to be true because it would likely land heavily on Chris's heart. "Your family is not going to change in the way you want. Instead of waiting on your mom to be who you want her to be, do what *you* can to change the pattern. There is an opportunity here to heal and set a new legacy in motion for our family."

Chris took a deep breath and said, "You're right that I so badly want my family to change. The little boy in me is still waiting for them to show up at the birthday party or around the tree on Christmas morning and my fantasy never comes true. It's draining. I want to stop spending so much of my energy on disappointment and regret, on waiting for something that isn't or won't be," His voice lightened slightly. "So, what do you suggest?"

"Well," I said, "before you can do it differently, it's important to get into a neutral headspace. To take a pause and recalibrate, so let's get outside and go for a walk."

Chris and I have always shared a love of walking. It's a fun and easy exercise and it also serves to clear our minds, to get in a space of neutrality. This is important. When we're neutral, we can be objective and discerning, rather than reactive and judgmental. As we walked along, Chris talked more about his family history and his desire to set a new pattern in motion. I encouraged him. "You can't 'fix' your parents, but you can heal yourself by giving your kids what you didn't get. This is a classic case of learning through opposites or contrast. When you know what you *don't* want, it allows you to really know what you *do* want. In your case, being the parent who shows up."

I walked him through an inventory exercise that's worked well for me and many of my clients.

"I start with where I am, with the feelings I'm wrestling with. In your case, you feel abandoned, orphaned. You don't feel worthy of receiving your family's attention, is that right?"

Chris nodded. "That about sums it up."

"Okay, next is visualizing or putting voice to where you want to be, how you *want* to feel."

"That's easy." He turned to me. "I want to be surrounded by family. Included. Embraced, like a group hug all the time."

I smiled, picturing all six of our kids throwing their arms around Chris. Most of our kids are tall, long-limbed teenagers who still hug Chris without hesitation, and little Haven loves her "Daddy sandwiches," as she calls them, where she and I both wrap our arms around him, smothering him with love and attention. I thought to myself, *Doesn't he realize he's* already *surrounded by family?* I asked, "Well, if a group hug is what you're after, are you willing to release some of your old hurt to feel it?"

"Worth a try. What I've been doing for fifty-three years hasn't worked so far," he relented with a smile. "To be clear: When you say 'release,' you mean that I have to let it go, right?"

"Not exactly. I'm saying that it may be time to accept your parents' shortcomings. That doesn't mean that you agree with their behavior, past, present, or in the future, only that you accept them as they are. And rather than regret or try to change the past, *focus forward*. Focus on what you can control—your own behavior."

By the time we returned to the house, Chris was in a much better mood. I could see it. What's more, I could feel it. The tension in the air had shifted toward playful and light. And when we opened the door, Haven ran into his arms and proclaimed without prompting, "You're the best daddy!"

I turned to Chris and whispered, "You're already doing it differently. Don't you see? You show up for your family one hundred percent. That's your superpower, your strength. And this one"—I nodded at Haven—"is learning from you. She happily shows up for you. With endless hugs."

QUESTIONS FROM THE FRONT ROW

Q: I'm not sure I understand the concept of "healing forward." Can you elaborate?

A: Healing forward begins with inquiry, where you ask yourself: How can I use my pain as an opportunity to do things differently in the future? Additionally, can I feel gratitude for the opportunity to be, act, and do it differently than generations before me? Can I feel gratitude for what I've already done to set a new loving legacy in motion that heals past wounds? Next, ask yourself: Can I be open to other people's healing energy as a way to heal forward? Whether we admit it or not, so many of us are guarded or are not receptive to outside help. What Spirit has taught me is that our relationships are intended to help us learn and grow, and in order to do so, we must be willing and courageous enough to let our guard down and open our hearts. The most healing relationships are those that strike a balance between independence and codependence. They are those that inspire and allow us to freely give to others without losing ourselves in the process, while maintaining a vulnerability and openheartedness to receive love in return. In this respect, the lesson I AM worthy + I AM here to heal are intertwined. It is only after we recognize and embrace our worthiness to receive love that we can truly heal forward. And when we allow others to love us, we provide a healing in return because the act of giving creates an energetic boost. When we accept love from the people in our lives who freely want to give it, both parties are lifted up to the highest vibrations of joy and gratitude.

Q: Is it sometimes the case that "healing" a relationship comes down to one person and not both people doing the work to heal?

A: At the heart of Chris's story is acceptance—accepting that we cannot force or will a healing in someone else. Chris was able to initiate a healing with his dad (page 25) because his dad took some ownership of his actions and how they affected his relationship with his sons. His mother, on the other hand, is not yet ready to take accountability, and until she's ready to do so, Chris's chances of healing their relationship are slim to none. The best that he can do is to surrender his expectations of her changing and to focus on what he can change. Himself. I refer to this process as: calling our energy *back* to heal *forward*.

This process can feel uncomfortable or even wrong, like we're giving up on something or someone. Chris certainly experienced some of this internal conflict. He still struggles with feeling guilty that he hasn't been able to "fix" his relationship with his mom. Most of us understand from experience that guilt is a tough feeling to wrestle with, but when we stop trying to fix or change people and evolve a sense of acceptance for what *is* and honoring the choices others make by exercising their free will, we're lifted energetically. Again, this doesn't mean that we agree with or like the choices of others, but our work is not to agree with other people's choices or to try and change them. The best we can do is to heal ourselves and to serve as an example to those around us, and this is often when change in others does happen. Where it may feel self-centered to focus solely on our own healing, this *is* the path to healing the people around us and the larger world. The importance of healing is not only about our own evolution but also about interdependence. Healing others connects us to the larger picture and anchors us back to the truth that we are all connected and not alone. Especially in our current and near-recent disruptive times marked by political strife, racial and gender targeting, war, and sickness, it is important that each one of us commits to healing ourselves individually and then, extending that healing outward. My Team Spirit has shown me a "line out the door" of souls trying to incarnate into our polarized and messy world, so if you're already here, consider it to be your proof that you have a unique purpose and contribution to make to the planet at this time.

Grow the Feeling through Inspired Action

• • •

Putting the I AM here to heal + contribute lesson into practice starts with exercising gratitude. Can you feel gratitude for the opportunity to do it differently than the generations that came before you did? Do you feel gratitude for what you've already done to set a new loving legacy in motion?

I want to let you in on another insight I've gained from the Other Side: when you feel gratitude for what's shown up in your life, and especially for the challenges that offer you an opportunity to break old patterns and focus forward, your energy will lighten. No kidding. Feeling gratitude is the fastest way to elevate your vibration. There's a reason why so many people have caught on to the gratitude journal trend: practicing gratitude moves mental and emotional blocks out of our way.

Remember, heaven is a state of mind, of being and feeling, and one we can ascend to in this life by appreciating what we have to work with. When we stop trying to control, resist, and fear the situations, circumstances, and relationships that have shown up in our lives, and instead express gratitude for the opportunity for growth, we begin to heal ourselves, our loved ones, and the world around us.

Part IV

Pick a Study Partner

CHAPTER 8

I AM Learning from Others
+ I AM Teaching Others

• • •

In late February 2021, I watched along with millions of other parents as Dr. Laura Berman, the relationship therapist, shared on *The Dr. Oz Show* the terrifying details of her son's accidental drug overdose and death. Her sixteen-year-old son, Sammy, a straight-A student excited about going to college, had unknowingly purchased counterfeit fentanyl-laced drugs and overdosed in his upstairs bedroom. Laura discovered him lying on his back, what is termed the fentanyl "death pose," because the respiration slows down to the point where the victim passes out. Laura recalled regretfully, "One of the silver linings of Covid's shelter-in-place restrictions was that I had all three of my boys at home where they were safe. I was wrong."

Watching the full interview with Chris, I felt a mother's fear rise up in me, unable to imagine Laura's loss and grief. I also felt an intuitive hit and turned to Chris and said, "I *know* Spirit wants me to work with her one day." Then, almost a year later to the day, Laura reached out to me on the recommendation of a longtime client of mine. She invited me to be a guest on her podcast, *The Language of Love,* and agreed to connect later via Zoom for a reading. Once we were on opposite screens, I said a quick silent prayer of protection and connection and asked Laura to say her name out loud three times. As soon as she did, I felt a rush of adrenaline as I clairvoyantly saw Sammy jumping up and down with excitement that he had Laura's full attention. In my mind's eye, I saw him standing next to a handful of her deceased family members and guides, ensuring me that he was in good hands. I felt clearly that this was Sammy, but just to be sure I asked him to confirm his presence and he showed me a butterfly.

"He's showing me a butterfly. Does that mean anything to you?"

"I see them all the time since his death," Laura choked out.

"He sends them to you," I said, "and he's here right now with your guardian angel and a spirit guide, an energy that feels maternal. I'm getting the sense that this guide is on assignment with you to help you through the painful loss of your son. The three of them are standing together, and now Sammy is showing me the scene of his death and he wants you to know that he didn't intend to overdose. He was curious and experimenting, trying temporarily to leave his body, which is why most people use drugs—to escape."

"It was the early days of Covid," Laura interjected, "and he was so bored at home. So many of the kids were, and I think he was just looking for something to *do.*"

"That's right," I confirmed. "He's showing me the moment he overdosed and he's floating above his body. He felt no pain, just confusion, wondering why his conscious awareness was still intact while he was detaching from his body. He started to freak out and resist when he realized what he'd done, and then the loving presence of a guide appeared by his side and held space for him while he was given a choice: let go and cross over or return back to his body with a near-death experience. He's showing me that he chose to turn his back and walk away, my "sign" for leaving the Earthly realm, because on a soul level Sammy felt that he'd already completed much of his work here and he had important work to do on the Other Side."

I paused as Sammy downloaded me with more information. He flashed an image of himself standing in the center of a group of taller boys. "Was he bullied?"

"Yes," Laura whispered.

"He's making me feel like fitting in socially was really hard for him."

"It was," Laura confirmed. "He was bullied terribly, and he so badly wanted to be accepted and included. He did finally find a group of kids who were nice to him, but they were into drugs. I remember when he asked my husband and me if he could try marijuana as a way to fit in, and I was glad that he'd come to us and I wanted him to have friends, but I just couldn't say yes to drugs so that his friends would accept him."

"I can feel him relating to me, drawing a parallel between the two of us. Like I am, Sammy was an empath and very sensitive. He struggled with the harshness of this world, overwhelmed by the energy of loud crowds and noise, and this is one of the reasons he gravitated toward drugs; he wanted to numb out from the world. If he had chosen to stay, he could 'see' that his life would have been a struggle, as he would likely be dealing with opioid addiction. He didn't want to burden you with this struggle."

"I've done my research and fentanyl is fifty to a hundred times more potent than morphine and three times as addictive as heroin," Laura offered, "and *highly* addictive. If you survive your first hit, you'll be addicted for life, which is why drug dealers push it on teens."

"He was very young to die," I empathized, "and yet, he's showing me a specific time line, flashing me the numbers sixteen, nineteen, and twenty-one, meaning that an early exit was inevitable if he bypassed this one."

"It's hard for me to believe that he was meant to go," Laura admitted. "Looking back, I can't help thinking: Was there anything I could have done to help him? To save him?"

"He's shaking his head. It's not your fault, and you couldn't have prevented it. You did everything in your power to be a present, loving, and hands-on mother. He's saying that this was his journey, his choices."

"How could he *choose* that? He was only sixteen, just a kid."

"You lost your son much sooner than you ever expected and you're still grieving so it's hard to see the bigger picture, but Sammy wants you to try and get out of your head and stop torturing yourself with all the 'what if's.' If you can move into acceptance of his free will, of his choice to pass on, this is the greatest way to honor his soul. He's showing me an umbilical cord to symbolize your connection that extends between this world and the next, always, and forever."

Laura was quiet for a moment and finally said, "I just want to *feel* him, to *know* he's there."

"With acceptance, the static in the line will clear and you'll be able to connect much better. While you've done a tremendous amount of work to heal your grief, it is still interfering with your connection."

I explained to Laura that energetically, grief and despair resonate on a lower frequency and spirits reside in the higher realm, so to connect with our departed loved ones, we must raise our energy to match theirs, which is exactly what I do to make connections with the Other Side.

"The reality is that you will grieve for a long time," I continued. "But to quote one of my favorite teachers, Elisabeth Kübler-Ross who wrote in her book *On Death and Dying:* 'You will not "get over" the loss of a loved one; you will learn to live with it. You will heal and you will rebuild yourself around the loss you have suffered. You will be whole again, but you will never be the same. Nor should you be the same nor would you want to.' If I may add to that—grief is not a linear process. It will come in waves, and as you continue to bravely lean in to your grief and consider the deeper meaning and lesson within the tragedy, you will start to feel better, incrementally. And over time you will feel more peaceful, more resolved, and that will raise your vibration such that you can better connect with Sammy. Although"—I smiled—"he's showing me that he's already nudging you, sending you signs, whether you know it or not."

"Like what?" Laura perked up.

"He's sending you white roses, which," I added, "vibrate at the frequency of forgiveness. He wants you to forgive yourself."

"Oh my gosh," Laura said. "Just this morning my husband and I were talking about the pink rosebush in our yard that—for no reason at all—bloomed *white* roses this year."

That's a sign from Sammy. "Is there anything you'd like me to ask him?" I offered.

"You said earlier that Sammy had already completed much of his work here and he had important work to do on the Other Side. What do you mean?"

I took a deep breath and asked: *Spirit, show me more.* In my mind's eye, I saw an open book on a podium, a sneak peek of Sammy's Book of Life.

"What I'm getting is that Sammy's soul—again, not his conscious mind or his sixteen-year-old human self, but his soul, his spirit—made the choice to move on to the higher realms because he felt that he could teach people in a bigger way, while collaborating with you as a silent partner on the ground. Does that make sense?"

"Sammy's story has changed the conversation around the opioid crisis so much already," she said. "I'm not sure I understand how we're working *together*," Laura admitted.

"Two of the biggest lessons we come to Earth to learn," I said, "are to value our inherent worth. To feel worthy of who we are, just as we are, as we were born. And to heal transgenerational wounds passed down through our family line. Since you, Laura, already have the influence and the platform to reach millions of people, Sammy can work with you now in spirit to help educate people about this growing epidemic that, in many ways, is a by-product of a collective sense of unworthiness. Why do so many kids turn to drugs? Because they feel like they don't fit in with other kids at school, with their families, with the larger, on-screen world where everyone is trying to feel relevant. My husband, Chris, and I observed this when we recently attended the music and arts festival Coachella. Everywhere you turned, so many young people posing for selfies, desperately seeking Insta-fame. I could feel the competition energy all over the place, which vibrates at the low frequency of scarcity and lack and makes us feel not good enough, pretty enough, funny enough, rich enough, popular enough, and on and on. When we don't feel good enough, we look for ways to fill the void, and I think Sammy, like so many kids his age, fell into this trap. You said that he was bullied, right?"

"Yes," Laura confirmed again and offered, "and he internalized the bullying. I saw him as perfect exactly as he was, and he saw something else—the flaws, what he thought was missing."

"Exactly, he didn't believe in his worthiness. He was suffering. And now, he sees what you saw in him, that his spirit is whole and perfect, and he wants to work with you to help other kids who are struggling and to help guide other parents to understand their children better and cultivate a sense of worth and acceptance of themselves just as they are."

I paused as I felt the energy of another spirit step forward. I sensed that it was mother energy. I asked, "Is your mother deceased?"

"Yes, she died ten years ago."

"She's here, too, and she's making me feel a pinch in my heart center, and I'm seeing a black blob over the chest area. Did she have breast cancer?

"She did, and a year after she died, I got breast cancer in my left breast, just as she did."

"Wow, okay, she's connecting the dots for me. There is a transgenerational pattern here of accommodating others, of overgiving. I see you with your arms outstretched, almost to the point of discomfort, as if to say, there's an output of care but no input. Does that make sense?"

"It does. Mom taught me that it was better to give than to receive, and I've always over-nurtured others while *under*-nurturing myself. When Mom was sick, I took care of her, and after she passed, I bypassed the pain. I just kept going, staying busy, not slowing down, and telling myself I didn't have time to grieve, and it wasn't until I got cancer that I had to totally stop my life and change how I was doing things to take care of my body and heal myself."

"Ahhh, I get it. This is another lesson about worthiness, *your* worth and self-care this time. She's showing me a pink, healthy heart that is pumping love, in and out of its main artery, as if to say that the work you did to heal your cancer helped to heal your mom's heart, too. And now, she and Sammy are standing together on the Other Side saying that your healing work will continue, for yourself and for others, so long as you keep your heart open."

A week after the reading, I reconnected with Laura on another Zoom call where she reported, "I'm just starting to understand the 'work' Sammy and I have to do together and how his death can be a catalyst for saving and healing lives. Beyond generating more awareness of the opioid crisis with our kids, I'm working on organizing grief retreats for other mothers who are stuck in their grief and pain, and I'm learning through this experience that our greatest purpose often comes out of what breaks our heart."

"I cannot imagine the heartbreak of losing a child," I offered Laura, "but remember: you and Sammy are forever intertwined, as teacher and student, backward and forward in time. And in this lifetime, you have joined together to do meaningful, purposeful work."

Group Assignment

• • •

In addition to choosing specific lessons to learn in this lifetime, we each chose a group of souls to enroll with in Earth School. Our "soul group" is ours alone and provides us with unparalleled opportunities to heal and grow throughout our lifetimes. Robert Schwartz mirrors this sentiment in *Your Soul's Plan*: "There is a powerful perspective we can embrace to find solace, acceptance, peace, self-compassion, and even liberation as we travel through life's peaks and valleys. This perspective is that we planned our own life—the parents we were born to, the relationships we engage in, even the challenges we face—to evolve as a soul ... [and] the pre-birth plan perspective also helps us to know that we never journey alone." Spirits who have crossed over and who now have that wider perspective understand that it is through our human relationships that we have the greatest potential for growth. Just as scrolling through images of your ideal beach vacation comes nothing close to actually digging your feet into the sand, we experience, feel, and learn so much more when we dig into relationships with other people. Sure, we can learn in isolation, but the important lessons that we've each been born into this life to tackle and complete are accelerated by our interactions and experiences with others. Instead of *speed dating*, our time here is better spent with others *speed learning*. As Laura and Sammy's story illustrates, our deepest relationships with those within our soul group have the power to completely blow our hearts wide open and transform our lives.

Based on what I've gleaned from Spirit, your "soul group" includes thousands of souls you've been connected to through multiple lifetimes, though you don't encounter them all at once. You are joined together to fulfill different roles for each other in the spirit of growth and transformation, often acting as mentors, counselors, and coaches. Borrowing again from classic school terminology, everyone in your soul group originated in the same "homeroom," and once that group is formed, it stays intact. Meaning that you will be connected to your classmates forevermore. Everyone is equal;

there are no "leaders" or "best of class." We may break into smaller study groups throughout our lives—we each learn and progress at different speeds—but we always return and regroup back *home.* Once again reunited in the spirit world, it's like a class party. The group celebrates those who graduated with honors while equally encouraging—no judgment, here!—those who have unfinished work to do. The group then decides who will be returning to Earth, who will be staying behind, and what roles everyone will play the next time around.

Still with me?

Let's take it up a level.

Dating back to my earliest meditations, when awareness of my heightened sensitivity to Spirit first began, I clairvoyantly "saw" three levels of soul groups. They appeared to me as bubbles within bubbles within bubbles, indicating a hierarchy of influence. When I later read *Journey of Souls* and *Destiny of Souls* by Dr. Michael Newton, I was blown away by how he similarly described soul groups based on thousands of patient accounts from their past life and life between life regressions.

The first grouping—your primary group—is made up of the souls you have a deep bond with, even if your interactions are limited or infrequent, like a friend you don't see very often. But when you do see that person, you feel an instant connection, as if no time has passed and no physical distance lies between you.

In general, think of your primary group as those people in your immediate family, your partner or spouse, your children, your closest friends and colleagues. If you have not experienced kind and compassionate relationships from people within your own family, it can feel especially difficult to trust the significance of these connections, so let your emotional reaction be your clue. The people who spark or trigger the strongest emotions within us, both positive and negative, are typically in our primary group.

It's also not uncommon for one parent, sibling, or child to be part of our primary group while the other parent, sibling, or child is not. For instance, you may have several children, and while you love and value them all, there's one with whom you may feel an unspoken bond or closeness. While you can't necessarily put your finger on it, he/she/they feel deeply familiar to you, which indicates a soul group recognition. An example of this is my good friend Kate, who is one of three sisters, all close in age. Though she and her siblings were all raised in the same home and have many shared interests, experiences, and memories, Kate and her younger sister, Jill, are like two peas in a pod, so close and so aligned. Kate has told me that she and Jill often admit to feeling guilty that they don't share the same closeness or connection to their third sister. "It's likely that you and Jill are soul mates—in this life and in lives past," I've offered as an explanation, "and it's nothing to feel guilty about." Our mind loves to judge and label how we feel about people as being right or wrong, good or bad. I've counseled many clients who have an intuitive feeling about being more or less connected to some family members, but the cultural idea that family ties are the strongest and most important creates guilt and shame that generates inauthentic performative behavior when we just don't *feel it* with some family members. The truth is that not everyone under our family umbrella is in our primary soul group, and there's nothing to apologize for.

Given these wild variables, our primary groups can range from as few as three to upward of twenty-five souls and is united by a shared lesson plan based on what the group most needs to learn as a collective. For example, *your* primary group may be working hardest on the lesson "I AM remembering" while *my* primary group might be tackling "I AM worthy." During your time in Earth's classroom, every member of your primary soul group is working on the same curriculum, at their own individual pace.

You can imagine your secondary group as students in neighboring classrooms and your tertiary, or third, grouping occupying mobile classrooms on the other side of campus. The people in your secondary group might include your high school sweetheart, a neighborhood friend, or a favorite pet during a significant chapter in your life. Your tertiary soul group members may include the barista at your local coffee shop who you once saw regularly, or a mentor or teacher who you knew for a short time. While you interact with these people less frequently than you do your primary soul group, they can still be influential and meaningful relationships that show up at specific times in your life to help you learn a valuable lesson. Where our primary groups tend to be relatively small, our secondary and tertiary groups can contain upward of one thousand souls working on a variety of lessons that we have the opportunity to learn from, if even for a very short time. This number may seem high, and yet when you think about all of the people over the course of your entire lifetime who have impacted, influenced, or touched you in some way, the number fits, doesn't it?

Because we're born with a form of spiritual amnesia, not only have we forgotten what we are (spirit energy in a body) and from where we came (the highest energy source in the universe), but we have also forgotten with *whom* we're meant to travel Earth's precarious roads while we're here. In most cases, we know who our parents are, but when it comes to choosing friends, partners, and close confidants, we rely on a combination of chance encounter and divine orchestration to be reunited once again with our soul group "classmates." Many we've likely met already, while some are still to come, and when our paths do cross, it is up to each of us to recognize and embrace them for what they can teach us or to help us learn in this lifetime.

A Season. A Reason. A Lifetime.

• • •

Daphne reserved a spot in one of my small-group readings after she heard me on a radio show. Two months later, she arrived at my office and ducked into the shared bathroom before the reading was scheduled to start. She heard a woman crying in the stall next to her, and when they both emerged, Daphne made eye contact with her and offered a brief smile. Not ten minutes later, they locked eyes again on my reading couch. I was able to connect with Daphne's brother, Jon, who'd recently died. I confirmed that even though he was a young forty-three when he suddenly passed, he wasn't in pain and their grandmother was there to meet him as soon as his soul left his body.

Daphne said, "He died with his eyes wide open, as if he was surprised, and now I believe he was in wonder at seeing my grandmother appear as an angel to take him to heaven."

I channeled Daphne's brother for a bit longer and then shifted my focus to Brianna, the woman Daphne had met in the bathroom. I saw Brianna's husband and spirit standing side by side with Jon, their etheric arms interlaced, my "sign" that they were at a parallel place in their soul's evolution, as were their two living loved ones sitting before me.

I smiled at Daphne and Brianna and said, "Your husband and

brother are hanging out, helping each other get familiar with the spirit world. They both died around the same age, and they found each other on the Other Side. They want you to know that they're okay, and that they've got each other's back in the spirit world."

Daphne and Brianna looked at each other with a new recognition and smiled, and an hour later, when the reading was over, I noticed Daphne and Brianna walk out together and exchange contact information, so I wasn't totally surprised when Daphne reached out to me a year or so later with the following email.

Hi, Rebecca,

That reading was an amazing day and a turning point in my spiritual life. Brianna and I (she's the woman whose husband died around the same time as my brother) started talking over the phone every Sunday night, as that was one of her toughest times of missing her husband. We called it the Sunday Night Blues and we've spent hours talking every week since about our spiritual lives and our search for answers and closure. From that single afternoon in your office, Brianna and I have built a friendship and I am convinced that we have known each other in past lives. People laugh at us when we say we are best friends even though we've only "met" that one time in Denver. The miracle of it all is that Jon's death didn't end my life. It blew open my soul and brought me to my best friend.

The connections we make with people aren't by chance. They surface in our lives for a reason and a season, and sometimes a lifetime, and whether you share love and laughter or hardship and struggle with a person, within these relationships are important lessons to be learned or taught. This is the essence of **Lessons 6 and 7:**

I AM learning from others and I AM teaching others.

Of course, not everyone you meet belongs to your soul group or has something to teach you. Many people wander in and out of our lives without impact, so if you want to know who has shown up to help you learn an important lesson, listen to your feelings. How do the people in your life make you *feel*?

Typically, our most fulfilling relationships inspire feelings of safety, confidence, worthiness, attractiveness, harmony, happiness, and deep connection. When we feel seen and heard, empowered, valued, and loved, or when we feel déjà vu, a strong sense of familiarity around a person that we can't shake or put our finger on (*Haven't we met somewhere before?*), you can be pretty sure you've reunited with someone from your soul group, or possibly a soul mate.

How Strong Is the Connection?

• • •

Energetically, we form etheric cords to other people—you can think of them as invisible umbilical cords. These cords vary in size and power, based on the significance of the soul connection. The cords that bind you to those in your primary group can be as thick as tree trunks, whereas the energetic cords that bind you to souls in your tertiary group can be as thin as dental floss. Contrary to what many dating sites espouse, most of us have more than one "soul mate," someone whom we feel deeply connected to in our primary group, and these relationships aren't necessarily romantic in nature (remember my friend Kate and her sister, Jill). In *What the Dead Have Taught Me About Living Well*, I shared the story of my divorce from my first husband, Brian, who I referred to as my soul mate for many years. When our happy union eventually dissolved, many people were left scratching their heads. They wondered: If Brian is your "soul mate" why would you break up?

The answer I provided then to my friends, family members, and many of my clients holds true today—Brian was and still is *a* soul mate. What spirits have shown me is that most of us have more than one soul mate in our lifetimes. At different points, we attract certain partners, friends, and mentors into our life experience or are drawn to others with whom we feel a deep closeness and connection, based on our emotional, physical, and spiritual needs at that time. Our soul mates serve to help us grow even when the relationship involves conflict or ends in separation. Every partnership holds significance and yet sometimes it must end to propel both people forward in life. Endings are new beginnings that are often beneficial to both people, if not immediately, then over time.

The truth is that our soul mate relationships can extend to our siblings, our children, and our parents and can be deeply challenging, rife with struggle, and marked by transgenerational wounds. And yet these soul mate relationships offer us the most powerful and life-changing opportunities to heal ourselves and help to heal others, backward and forward in time.

Change the Narrative

• • •

If you're struggling in a relationship with someone that leaves you feeling taken advantage of or powerless in some way, reframe the relationship in the following way:

I am oppressed and controlled by others. I am a victim. ⇨

I AM learning from others.

If you're struggling in a relationship with someone, or more than one person, who leaves you feeling unimportant or ignored, reframe the relationship in the following way:

I am inconsequential and irrelevant to others. ⇨

I AM teaching others.

Spirits have shown me that within our soul group we often play opposite roles to one another to foster learning and growth. In some relationships we are the student and in others we are the teacher, and sometimes we are both. And get this—we often role-reverse and gender-reverse from one lifetime to the next to speed up the learning process. Meaning, your mother in this life may be your daughter in the next. Or your best girlfriend today may have been your brother in a past life. I know this sounds like *Freaky Friday* stuff, but in readings, spirits frequently identify the different roles they've played across lifetimes with their still-living loved ones, like the best friends who say they've always "felt like sisters" because, as it turns out, they were biological sisters in another incarnation! It was clear to me in the reading with Laura Berman that she played the role of "teacher" to Sammy for the years leading up to his death and now, in spirit form, Sammy has assumed the role of teacher on the Other Side from where Laura is now learning from him.

Role reversals can resolve generational wounds and create balanced karma between two souls. As a medium, it's so cool to witness these *aha* moments when I'm able to help clients connect the dots and understand why they assume the role or behave in a certain way around someone in their soul group.

For example, I recently welcomed Kaitlin and her seven-year-old daughter, Emma, into one of my virtual small-group readings. Straightaway, a male spirit stepped forward and identified himself as their husband and father, respectively. Ted showed me that he'd died of a heart attack, and I sensed that he was much older than his wife. He confirmed my intuition by flashing an image of Paul Newman in my mind's eye, my "sign" for an attractive and vibrant older man.

Kaitlin laughed and confirmed that he was in his early seventies when he passed, and that people often remarked that he looked like Paul Newman! This was his second marriage, and even though Kaitlin was twenty-five years younger, she felt that they were soul mates.

"Why is he showing me a monkey?" I addressed Emma directly. "He's making me feel like this message is specifically for you."

Emma teared up and said, "That was his nickname for me, 'little monkey,' and also, he painted a mural of monkeys on my bedroom wall."

"This is his way of showing you that he is still here with you." I turned to Kaitlin and said, "Ted is flashing the number range seventy to seventy-two, indicating that he was meant to leave this world somewhere between those ages, shortly after Emma was born. And he's also showing me the image of Emma positioned at the top of a pyramid to indicate that even though your daughter is only seven, she came into this life to play protector and caregiver to *you*, knowing that the probability of your husband's passing was very high."

This mother-daughter duo smiled at each other. Kaitlin said, "Well, that sounds about right. Since she was about three, she's told me that she was sent by angels to take care of me."

"My daughter, Haven, has said the exact thing to me!" I remarked. "And to confirm this, your husband is flashing an image of the two girls side by side to validate that Emma and Haven have a similar soul contract, and he's also making me feel that Emma has played this role before, acting as a mother figure to you in past lives, as well."

Kaitlin's smile widened. "Ted and I used to joke that she was the real mama in charge and wise far beyond her years."

"This should serve as validation that Emma really was sent by angels to help you get through this painful and difficult time of losing your husband. I can feel that you both miss him greatly, and that even though Emma is the younger of you two, she is incredibly strong and resilient, and she will serve to remind you that Ted is still present with one foot firmly planted in this world to watch over you both."

"I have dreams about him!" Emma excitedly interjected. "He tells me that everything will be okay."

"And it will." I smiled. "He's showing me that he will continue to visit both of you in your dream state as a way to stay connected to him. He also wants me to bring up your father, Kaitlin. Is he still alive?"

She nodded. "Yes, but we've had our differences and we're currently not speaking."

"Well, Ted is making me feel that your dad has been stubborn and owes you an apology and that you'll be hearing from him one day soon. Ted is using his influence on the Other Side to prompt your dad to reach out. And when he does, Ted is asking you to thank your dad for playing the role of "teacher," providing you with an important opportunity to learn the lesson of forgiveness. If you accept his apology, you can check that box off your list."

I could feel Kaitlin's resistance to this particular message, along with a heavy dose of skepticism. I didn't push it. I let it go, trusting that it would play out in the right time. And the very next day I received this email from Kaitlin:

> In my reading with you yesterday, my father came up and you said that if I heard from him, he would give me an apology. Honestly, in 48 years I have never received one [from him], so I was extremely skeptical. Well, I got a text *this morning* from my dad saying that he could not be more ashamed for the way he's acted over the years. You were right. Great job, Ted!!

This nearly immediate nudge from Spirit was exactly what Kaitlin needed to help her shift away from doubt toward the higher vibration of faith and trust, acceptance and forgiveness.

Q: As parents, aren't we meant to teach our kids, and not the other way around? Why would we agree prebirth to this role reversal? It feels counterintuitive to most parenting advice, and I don't want to be a bad parent.

A: Our children are spiritual beings on their own unique path. When it comes to soul contracts, whether it's a parent-child, sibling-sibling, or anything else, physical age is an illusion; just because one is older in Earth years does not necessarily mean they/he/she is an older soul or that they're more evolved on a spiritual level. Simply, age alone does not make one wiser. In readings, both maternal and paternal spirits will often refer to their living children as the older or more advanced soul whose role was, and still *is*, to play teacher to them, a role they asked them to play. While they had no conscious awareness of this agreement when they were alive, these spirits realize on the Other Side that their child was acting as a mirror to them to help them learn and grow. It is true that as Earth parents, it is our responsibility to care for our children physically and emotionally by keeping them safe, extending our love, and providing them with an important moral compass to help them navigate life. But we must recognize that our children are not secondary to us in the greater hierarchy, and we aren't in charge at the soul level. We must have the humility to step back and open ourselves to the possibility that they are here to teach us the important life lessons we signed up to learn.

As I've shared earlier, I didn't always feel seen or heard in my house while growing up. My parents did their best, but they easily became distracted by their own inner dialogues, and I could sense when they were only half there, not fully listening, their minds elsewhere. When I became pregnant with my first child, I conjured that feeling of dismissal and absence and made a silent promise to Jakob that I would be different. I would be an attentive, present parent. Lesson lived and learned.

Well, what can I say? My actions have fallen short; I'm not always present in the parenting department. My sons Jakob and Sam generously give me a pass, but Haven doesn't let me slide through Earth School. The other night as I was putting her to bed, I asked her: "What was the best and the worst thing that happened today, and what is something you're excited for tomorrow?"

As she began to relay the details of her day, sharing how a classmate who cut in front of her in the lunch line was the worst part of her day and snuggling up with me was the best thing, my phone pinged with a new message. I automatically pulled it out of my pocket, and as I did, Haven put her hand over my phone and said, "Mama, how 'bout you put your phone down and listen to me?" Busted!

And she was right to school me in that moment. My lesson is to be present, to heal my childhood wound of feeling dismissed and to heal forward, to create a new, healthier pattern for my own children. I tucked my phone away and thanked my beautiful and wise daughter for being my teacher.

Until We Meet Again

• • •

Often the hardest part of reuniting with soul mates on Earth is letting them go when it's their time to return back home. When a soul mate dies, it can feel like a part of us has died as well. After all, we are energetically intertwined (remember the invisible cord?). To cope with the pain of such a loss, we may disassociate from our bodies to escape, or numb the pain to avoid or completely "void" what we're feeling.

Dissociation is a term that indicates disconnection from one's own self; it is a common, though largely unconscious, response to stress and trauma. On the mild end of the spectrum, we may operate as if on autopilot, going through the motions of life while not being fully present or aware of what's happening around us. It's the experience of being there but not there. We may dissociate at odd times, like when we're in the middle of an argument or midway through a meal. In its extreme state, disassociation is the experience of disconnecting from the body as a form of self-protection and survival and is related to the body's physiological stress response. Dissociation can become an unhealthy pattern that takes a toll on our nervous system and overall sense of safety and well-being.

Disassociation can also lead to spiritual bypassing, a method of hiding behind spirituality or spiritual practices rather than acknowledging and embracing our true feelings and shadow side. To bypass is tempting, but in order to reconcile any significant loss, we must first feel into our dark and messy and uncomfortable feelings without judgment and resist the temptation to dismiss the pain with conclusions like "everything happens for a reason," "there's a lesson in this," "it's a blessing in disguise," "it's all part of Spirit's plan." While these conclusions may be true, eventually, we must first lean in to the darkness before we can heal and return to the light. Only after we wrestle with the shadows can we then uncover the deeper meaning, lesson, or purpose behind the experience.

In readings, spirits discourage their living loved ones from dissociating in this way and encourage them to return to their present-day lives, where they can focus on completing their life assignments and find a greater sense of purpose. Spirits also remind the living that we are eternally bonded as souls within the same soul group and we will one day be reunited again. Until then, they encourage the living to ask for signs, synchronicities, and dream visitations to instill deeper trust that our soul mates are energetically with us until we finish out our lifetime.

This next story about Mike and Ann is a perfect illustration of this. My client Ann lost her husband, Mike, after more than thirty years of marriage. Though the loss was profoundly painful, and she did "disassociate" for a period of time, she was finally able to move forward by trusting in a connection that transcends the physical world. With her permission, I'm including her story here, told in her own words.

The love of my life, my husband, passed away tragically and unexpectedly on Valentine's Day. Mike was an amazing man, and his love for me, and our two beautiful daughters, was evident every single day. We shared a level of comfort with each other that was rare. There were many times in our life together when I could sense him, feel him, smell him as if he were right next to me yet we were not even in the same town. It was as if a part of me was always with him and vice versa. We were meant to be.

When we got news of his passing I was thrown into a tail-spin of shock and disbelief. It was an abyss of nothingness. I can only describe it as deep, deep emptiness, a huge dark black hole, which then became deep pain and intense grief. An unfamiliar place. I was lost, broken, alone, physically and emotionally sick. I felt empty. I could not breathe, and I had no desire to eat. I felt as though I did not belong in this world. I did not want to live. Every breath and every step was a chal-lenge, and none of it felt right. I was paralyzed by grief. I was trying to understand my feelings and emotions, but I felt like I was not truly here. I had not experienced death, but in a way, I felt dead, and I wanted to be with Mike. My life now seemed like a strange land, and death seemed the easier road. Only my physical self was here, as my heart and soul had gone with Mike.

I always had the feeling that our loved ones never leave us, but now it was necessary for me to truly *know this*, not just think or believe it. I scheduled a reading with Rebecca for me and my two daughters. I don't even remember how I did it, but we got one. We were scheduled in June, just four months after Mike's passing. This was our first ever reading, and we were all very emotional. We really did not know what to expect. A male spirit came in very strong along with the name "Mike" and his first message was about the "tree." He shared with Rebecca that he'd had a heart attack while in the mountains and passing near a tree. Validation! I had not told her this. He said that the last thing he wanted was to not be here physically but that he was energetically connected to all three of us. "Cemented to our energy until it was our time to cross over" were his words. He also referenced a previous life where he and I had been

222 · What's Your Heaven?

connected as husband and wife, and I had died first, and it was all part of the plan, our "soul contract," to role reverse in this lifetime. There was a reason behind his early death, and we could've done nothing to prevent it. And now, my daughters and I were meant to help bring closure to his physical death and help each other heal. Everything we loved about him—his spirit, his kindness, his essence, his true personality, and especially his love for us—was still alive and would always be with us. Keep inviting him in every day, he said, and he would do his best to show up through signs and connections. He explained that we were soul mates and when he died a part of me died, and now, I had to call my soul back to me so that I could begin to live in this world again and to help our daughters. Rebecca explained that we would never have to go through something this heartbreaking again, and whether we chose to stay in Spirit or incarnate again, we are a team, we are not done, and we will never be done.

I still have dark, hard moments and days when I miss Mike deeply and I know I always will while I'm still here in a body. But I have learned to try and accept it all and to trust, to be open to receiving all of the healing energies and guidance from the Other Side that remind me we are not meant to do it alone, and to acknowledge the kindness of those here on Earth who have helped me and my family. Every day I work on honoring my own spirit. It is not an easy journey, but I find peace and comfort in the knowing that I am forever connected to Mike.

Homework

· · · ·

WHAT'S THE LESSON?

Identifying the people in your life who may or may not be in your soul group is fascinating stuff, but the true awakening comes when you understand what they've shown up to teach you and, in turn, what you've shown up to teach them. Truly, the key to satisfaction and fulfillment, closure and peace with our friends, family, colleagues, and loved ones, is to understand why we've shown up for each other. Once we have a better understanding of what we are bringing to the relationship on a higher, and often unconscious, level, we can begin to see how our deepest and often most challenging relationships serve as an opportunity to teach and to learn important lessons.

While Mike and Ann's relationship is a love story, its ending was heartbreaking and traumatic for Ann. As you do this next homework assignment, take an inventory of the relationships in which you feel deeply connected and where you may also have unresolved trauma, conflict, strain, or struggle. This may be a relationship with a child, partner, boss, colleague, siblings, parent, or dying parent. Consider your relationships with the living *and* the dead. Some of our more challenging relationships are with those who have passed on. I encourage you to dig into the relationships that are fraught because they tend to have the greatest lessons for us. Pay attention to feelings like resentment, anger, guilt, regret, shame, and fear, along with negative reactions like blaming, defensiveness, and holding grudges.

If you could assign a *feeling* to how you experience your most challenging or strained relationships, what would it be? _____.

What are the themes, patterns, struggles that keep repeating themselves in your most challenging relationships? Emotional reactions to people are often unhealed or unresolved aspects within us, and they are serving as a mirror, reflecting a wound, showing us a lesson to be learned. Simply put, when people trigger us, it's *our* stuff, not theirs, and a word of caution: what we resist, persists. When we don't heal these wounds, they keep cracking open. For example, if you feel like your romantic partners, one after the next, don't honor and respect you, take an honest look in the mirror. Do you respect and honor yourself? Or if you feel overlooked at work, consistently passed over by your colleagues for promotions and pay increases, consider your internal worth. Do you feel worthy of abundance? Trust that the pattern playing out in front of you is by design. It is an invitation to heal a wound that was created in this lifetime or has resurfaced from a past lifetime, and to heal it will bring balance back to your family line. Let's dig a little deeper and name a specific dynamic.

Name a recurring challenge/struggle/unresolved hardship/pattern or dynamic with a person/people: _____.

Zoom out and consider the agreement you made with this "classmate" back in the homeroom. What are the roles you are playing with each other in this lifetime? What can this dynamic teach you? For the moment, set aside blame, shame, grudges, and resentment. Reframe and rewrite the relationship struggle as a growth opportunity: _____.

For example, my tendency to automatically say yes in an effort to people-please makes me feel taken advantage of and, ultimately, resentful. When I reframe it, I see this struggle as an opportunity to set healthy boundaries and grow my self-respect.

My friend Amy was in a spin cycle of frustrating relationships with one boyfriend after another. Her habit of complaining about their inadequacies and then pushing them away resulted in short-lived relationships that never achieved a level of authentic intimacy. When she took the time to consider the lesson she had to learn, she recognized that these relationships were showing up to mirror her own feelings of inadequacy. After she wrestled with her shadow side, she connected with her vulnerability. As she bravely revealed her imperfections to others, she began to experience true intimacy and compassionate relationships that endured.

My client Suzy had a pattern of being hypercontrolling, especially when it came to her children. She would micromanage every detail of their lives, despite their objections and rebellion. As she eventually came to realize, with some help from Spirit, at the heart of her behavior was a fear of abandonment and powerlessness. Her kids, all of whom are in her primary soul group, were simply playing out their roles to help Susie learn the humbling lesson of surrender. Eventually, Suzy was able to recognize the recurring dynamic and shift her reaction to a healthier response. She began to empower her kids to make their own choices by letting go of her fear-based inclination to control.

What do all of these examples have in common? While the types of relationships vary, each of these individuals were able to make positive shifts in their lives by recognizing the lesson within the context of their relationships. When we step out of reactivity, we begin to see that the people who trigger us the most can help us recognize and heal something within ourselves. Once we peek behind the curtain, so to speak, we can move away from defensive reactivity to an acknowledgment that our relationships, even the most challenging ones, serve to help us learn and grow in profound ways.

Extra Credit

Journal Underneath the Conflict

Sometimes we don't know exactly what's driving our reaction to the people in our lives. We just know that we don't feel good. Remember that a negative emotional charge in reaction to someone's behavior or actions points to something unhealed within ourselves that is calling for our attention. It's a clue. But if the clue is leading you in mental circles, try putting pen to paper. When I'm confused, I dump my feelings and knotted thoughts onto the page. The simple act of journaling can work to put the final puzzle pieces together. Review your life in relationship to others with the following prompts. Write down any feelings and thoughts that come up.

- What do you regret having done or not done in relationships with others?

- If you could change anything about your relationships, what would you change?
- Who do you have unresolved issues with, living or in spirit?
- *I'm sorry, I love you, please forgive me. Thank you.* Who in your life, living or in spirit, would you like to say these words to?
- Who would you like to apologize to? What would you say?
- Who do you wish would apologize *to you*, and for what?
- Who in your life triggers you most? What is the triggering behavior and how does it make you feel?
- Who has served as your greatest teacher, living or in spirit, offering you an example of how you *do* and *don't* want to live your life?

BONUS questions for accelerated learning

- What are the positive and negative relationship patterns that you inherited from your family?
- Of these patterns, which ones have you perpetuated in your lifetime?
- Knowing what you know now, what is the legacy—what are the lessons—you want to pass on to your friends, family, and children?

Bless the Mess

• • •

The people in our life are not happening to us, but *for* us. When challenging people or relationships show up in your life, consider: What is this relationship meant to teach me? Silently bless the mess, as I like to say, and ask your Team Spirit to help you see what's really at play. How can this challenging relationship help me grow?

This was the advice I shared with Lisa, a client wrestling with a soul mate relationship. She sought clarity about a man whom she believed would be in her life forever but who chose to end the relationship. They'd recently separated, and she was devastated. Her spirit guides validated her pain and acknowledged that her feelings for this man were not misplaced or "wasted." In fact, the message I received was that he'd come into her life to make a big impact, if only for a finite period of time. The purpose of his presence, and the intensity of their brief relationship, was meant to jump-start her heart.

"I'm seeing armor over your chest, indicating that you were closed off to relationships before this one and he blew your heart back open."

"Blew it open and broke it, is more like it," Lisa said.

"And while a broken heart takes time to heal and you're currently grieving, your guides are saying that this relationship was not meant to be forever. It was meant to represent promise and possibilities for the future by breaking you open so that your love could flow freely again, and so long as you stay open to receiving, and resist your natural urge to shut down, you will, in time, attract another relationship of equal or greater value. My sense is the next one will be explosive," I said. "In the best way."

Exercise
Wash Yourself with Pink

As you begin to embrace the truth that your soul group relationships are intentional, and especially the tough ones, run the color pink throughout your body to raise your energy. I've specifically chosen pink for this exercise because it is commonly interpreted as the color of relational, Earthly love and it vibrates at the high frequency of harmony, which is incompatible with oppression and the low vibration of victim consciousness and powerlessness. You will run pink through your system to release this shadow energy and spark the energy of openness and trust. When we shift our energy out of fear and doubt and remember that the people in our lives are happening for us instead of *to* us, we can get back into alignment with Spirit and attract high-frequency people and experiences into our lives.

Close your eyes and take several deep breaths to ground you in the present moment. Sit up straight with your feet on the ground and your hands resting in your lap. Pull your shoulder blades back, drop them down, and push your heart forward. With each breath, focus on relaxing your entire body, from the top of your head down through your feet. Once you feel centered and grounded, imagine a beam of golden white light extending up and through your crown chakra, moving past this dimension, into the higher frequencies of the heavenly realm and connecting you to Spirit.

Next, focus on your feet and envision another beam of golden white light extending from the sole of each foot that travels deep down into the Earth's soil, and farther down into the Earth's core.

Once you feel connected above and below, move your attention to your heart center. Place your hand over your heart as you visualize a spark of pink light begin to glow and grow there. Take notice of the shade of pink you're seeing or sensing, without judgment, trusting that whatever shade it might be is the perfect pink frequency you need at this moment. Continue to breathe. With each inhalation, visualize this pink light pumping your strong and steady heart. As it grows more and more intense, draw it in with each breath. Feel the light expand, loosen, open, and unblock your heart, allowing for resistance to dissipate. Breathe deeply and easily. (Again, if visualization is a challenge for you, use your physical senses. Try holding a rose quartz crystal in the palm of your hand, focus on the petals of a pink rose placed in front of you, or pour yourself a glass of pink lemonade.) Get creative, and once you have a mental picture or a visual representation of pink light running through you, tap at least three times on the karate chop point from the diagram on page 78. As you tap, repeat any of the following phrases that particularly resonate with you, either repeating the same or different phrases each time. Remember, the phrase names the fear or the struggle and is followed by an I AM statement of acceptance.

- Even though I feel oppressed by others . . . I AM leaning in to how I feel and I AM open to learning from them now.
- Even though I feel diminished by others . . . I AM giving myself permission to feel how I feel, knowing I AM worthy of love and respect.
- Even though I feel hurt by others . . . I trust that I AM deeply loved and it is safe to open my heart.
- Even though I feel aggravated by and resentful of others . . . I trust that I AM learning important lessons.

- Even though I feel some resistance to learning from X
  (name the person or situation) . . . I AM willing to change
  my mind about it and "see" that person or situation as an
  opportunity for growth.
- Even though a part of me doesn't want to learn this lesson
  . . . I AM accepting myself and how I feel.
- Even though I am resisting my role as a teacher . . . I AM
  willing to help/support/share my story with others.
- Even though I feel inadequate as a teacher . . . I AM
  accepting myself and trusting that I AM meant to play this
  role.

After tapping on the "karate chop" point, follow with a round or two of *feeling* statements that affirm the truth of how you feel. As you tap on the remaining eight meridian points—starting at the eyebrow point and ending at the top of the head—express whatever thoughts or feelings that come up for you. It could be a single word . . . "resistant," "frustrated," "hurt" . . . or even a single sound, or a long exhale.

Finally, follow with another full round of tapping on all eight meridian points, while repeating the I AM statements again:

- I AM leaning in to how I feel and I AM open to learning
  from them now.
- I AM giving myself permission to feel how I feel, knowing I
  AM worthy of love and respect.
- I trust that I AM deeply loved and it is safe to open my
  heart.
- I trust that I AM learning important lessons.

- I AM willing to change my mind about it and "see" that person or situation as an opportunity for growth.
- I AM accepting myself and how I feel.
- I AM willing to help/support/share my story with others.
- I AM accepting myself and trusting that I AM meant to play this role.

As you tap on the meridian points while repeating the I AM statements, ask your Team Spirit to help you shift and uplift your energy out of illusion and delusion, out of the shadows of victim consciousness and into the higher vibrational frequencies of forgiveness, acceptance, trust, and neutrality.

Continue to breathe IN: I AM. Breathe OUT: here to learn. Breathe IN: I AM. Breathe OUT: here to teach.

Lessons in Letting Go

• • •

In one of my small-group readings, two unrelated women, Kelly and Joy, voiced a similar struggle in their romantic relationships. This is not uncommon. Because spirits can maintain their presence in the dense energy of Earth's 3D world for only a limited amount of time, they will often deliver parallel messages to the group as a way to cover the course material most efficiently, so to speak. In this particular group, it became clear to me that both Kelly and Joy were in the process of expanding their "I AM here to learn + teach" awareness. They both expressed that they were currently on "different pages" from their partners, and I understood this to mean that they were no longer energetically matched to their partners. Spirit confirmed this by showing me a radio dial set to two different frequencies, 98.5 and 101.3, my "sign" that they were not attuned. Both Kelly and Joy voiced fear and trepidation about how to handle their mismatched relationships, and their guides stepped forward with a similar message: be true to yourself. What Spirit has shared with me over the years is that sometimes we get out of energetic alignment with our partners, and rather than try to match them by lowering to their level, or attempting to raise them to our vibration, it is our work to hold steady in ourselves. Anything less is a betrayal of self. And continuing down that destructive path does not serve you or your partner.

There is always some resistance to this message when it comes through because it is human nature to fear the unraveling of a significant relationship, and it is at this delicate moment when I gently ask: What will you *gain* by holding tightly to your current relationship? What will you *sacrifice* by holding tightly to your current relationship? If sacrificing your self by dimming your light, diminishing, or shrinking down to meet your partner is your answer, pay close attention to that. Spirit warns that self-sacrifice is the ultimate act of self-betrayal and often results in our own depletion, both physically and spiritually. On the other hand, when we bravely shift our focus away from making the dynamics of our relationships "work" (which can sometimes feel like forcing a square peg into a circle) and instead honor our self-worth, our energetic expansion, and our growth, we will either inspire our partners to rise up, or they will fade out if they are not a vibrational match to our frequency. This is true for friendships, romantic relationships, work relationships, and family relationships. Spirit has shown me that when we rise up into our higher self, we are joined by others in our soul group who are a match. Danielle MacKinnon phrases it this way in her book *Soul Contracts*: "Each person who leaves your life as a result of your soul system work will open up a space for a new person who matches the new vibration you hold."

QUESTIONS FROM THE FRONT ROW

Q: What if I'm willing to "rise up" and grow and my partner isn't?

A: I get this question a lot. It can feel disappointing if you're doing your work, and your partner isn't showing up to class. Again, the thing to remember is that you're only in control of your own choices and behavior. Even when you've made a soul agreement with another person to learn and grow together, you are responsible only for your part in the deal, and if your partner is unwilling to do his or her work, then you are free to move on to a new "study partner." In readings, Spirit will communicate this message by showing me a hot-air balloon that's ready to ascend. The sandbags holding it in place represent the people whom we're entangled with and who are energetically weighing us down, who are no longer on our level, or who are simply embarking on a different journey of their own. We should each feel free to cut loose those people who aren't ready to climb aboard with us. Remember that we form etheric cords to people that vary in size and power based on the significance of the soul connection. Sometimes these cords can begin to feel like hooks that drain and deplete our energy. When we symbolically cut and release cords with others who energetically weigh us down, we will naturally ascend to a higher place where we can soar. (And, to confirm the truth of this spirit wisdom, on my drive home from the office, right after writing this, I pulled behind a car with a custom license plate that spelled: SOAR!)

On a birthday weekend getaway with my best friend, Katie, she described a recent "hot-air balloon" situation in her own poetic way:

> It can be difficult to let go of relationships that once felt fulfilling. Releasing loved ones from your life because you're no longer a match (and not always realizing this is what's happening, just knowing that you're not "vibing" the way you used to) can feel awkward, uncomfortable, or sad. Often the other person doesn't understand why you're pulling away. As a result, they can get irritated, talk poorly about you to others, or be cruel and unkind. These are all just results of the painful rejection they might be feeling. But in my experience, if you gracefully evolve up and out of that connection, with compassion and kindness for both of you, then the "letting go" can happen with the least amount of destruction to the relationship. When you let go in this way, you can go your separate ways feeling nothing but love for each other and gratitude for the relationship you once shared.

Beautifully said—though, of course, this is easier said than done. But staying in a relationship to the detriment of your soul expansion is not truly living or loving, nor is it the legacy you want to leave behind. You owe yourself and the other person in the relationship much more than that. My first husband, Brian, and I struggled for many years to save our marriage because we thought it was the right thing to do. But after many hours in counseling, we eventually came to the same conclusion: we had learned important lessons from each other, we'd fiercely loved each other, and now, it was time to let each other go. Spirits come through in readings every day to nudge their living loved ones to similarly "learn and let go." Sometimes couples are able to change and grow within the marriage, but in our case, we understood that our work together was complete. And still, our eventual divorce didn't discount the years we'd spent together or what we'd learned from and taught each other in this lifetime. I'm grateful for the role Brian played in my life, and soon after we cut the energetic cords between us, we each embarked on new relationships with others from our soul group to learn and master new lessons.

My second husband, Chris, has taught me and continues to teach me the importance of measuring success in increments of joy rather than in dollars earned, or how many billable hours we collectively work. We have taught each other the importance of keeping "love on top" by making it a priority to spend quality alone time together away from work demands and the responsibility of six kids between us. Every couple of months, even if only for one day, we allow ourselves the time to reconnect, and this time together continues to teach me the importance of holding space for the other person to pursue the things that lift that person's energy, in a way that doesn't compromise my own. And, finally, we have similar work to find "the middle path," as it is referred to in Buddhism. We keep each other in check as we each seek to maintain balance in our lives rather than going to extremes, whether it's at work or at play. We're still actively learning this lesson. It's a work in progress!

Q: Beyond our primary soul groups, what about the people who come into our lives for a very short time? What are they here to teach us?

A: Sometimes the nurse at your doctor's office, your plumber, or your landlord are just people in your life, like extras on a movie set that appear in only one scene. And sometimes the people who occupy these roles in our lives have something important to teach us—or we may have something important to teach them. Remember that beyond your primary soul group, the people in the secondary and third groupings can still be influential, showing up at a specific time in your life with a meaningful message. As with any relationship, it's critical to tune in to how you *feel* around them. Your heart is your best guide here, not your mind.

For example, when Brian and I were wrestling with the decision to end our marriage, I had a dream visitation from my dad. In the dream, he reminded me that life is meant to be joyful and heavenly, and that perhaps it was time to honor our own paths and let each other go. He basically came through to validate what Brian and I had concluded on our own. Well, just days later, Richard, the landlord at my office building, got into the elevator with me. I didn't run into Richard often, but we were always friendly to each other. There was something familiar about him. Actually, he kind of reminded me of my dad. On the ride up to my floor, he asked me if everything was okay, and I involuntarily burst into tears. He walked me into my office foyer, and we ended up talking for thirty minutes. I opened up about my unraveling marriage and he listened, holding space for me like an old friend and a father figure rolled into one. As I talked to Richard, I felt even more clear that divorce was the right, yet difficult, decision to make.

As a thank-you for his attention and care, I offered Richard a reading right there on the spot, in which his father-in-spirit came through loud and clear, flashing my dad's birthday, 12–14, in my mind's eye. Richard confirmed that December 14 was *his* dad's birthday as well. No kidding! And as if he heard us talking about him, my dad pushed into the reading, along with Richard's mother-in-spirit, named Ruth (another synchronicity: my grandma Babe's real name was Ruth!), confirming that *his* people had called *my* people, and they were all working together to orchestrate this chance, and very cool, encounter. I understood that Richard was unconsciously acting as my teacher and guide that day, bolstering my courage and validating the next big step in my life. A few months later, I moved out of that office space and lost contact with Richard. I didn't forget him, though, nor have I dismissed the significant role he played in my life that afternoon.

Extending Beautiful Lessons

• • •

Many of the people in our lives show up to teach us, and in return, we are often acting as the teacher, guide, or messenger to others, whether we realize it or not. This next story is an illustration of how we can unconsciously sign up for a challenging soul contract that will serve to teach others an important life lesson. In the case of this soul, she incarnated into the severely deformed body of a young girl who died at age fifteen. The story was delivered to me from her great-uncle and my client, Albert, who has heightened intuitive skills himself. He sent me the following email about a dream visitation he had from his great-niece, whom he'd never met in life, nor was he aware of her death at the time of his dream. In Albert's words:

This very special dream took place when I least expected it. In [the dream], I am walking into a large living room space with people all around, like a family gathering. As I walk into the center of the room, I notice a beautiful young girl. She's radiant; her beauty is simply not normal. She's the most beautiful girl I've ever seen. I imagine her to be fourteen or fifteen years old. As I approach her, she looks up with a grin and says, "Hi, I knew you would come to see me. I was waiting for you."

I am surprised. I don't understand, and I look behind me to see if she is talking to someone else. I have no idea who this beautiful girl is. She can see that I am confused and gives me a big smile and says, "I am talking to you. I had been waiting for you. I am glad you came to see me. I invited you to come here to talk to me. Please listen carefully to me. My family will soon come to visit you and I need you to do something for me. I want you to tell them that I am in the right place now. I am beautiful now. I am finally free, and my beauty finally came out.

"I understand why it needed to happen. I know it seemed sad, but now I know it was very important for my soul and spiritual growth. Please, please pay attention to me now."

She stands up and makes this motion with her hair. She swings her body side to side, and her long brown hair flies in front of me, and she slides her hand through her scalp and says, "I wanted to do this all my life. Now I am strong, feeling wonderful and happy. I am free to move, to see, to sing and talk with my real voice. I know you might not be able to understand this, but you need to remember what I am saying and tell my family"

I am so confused. All I can say is, "Your family? I do not know you. I do not know your family. I do not even know where I am."

Once again, she giggles and says, "You look just like my grandfather. Trust me. You will know soon enough as to who I am and who my family is. Remember what I tell you now. They will come and visit you soon and you are my connection. Please just do your best and remember what I tell you." She giggles again and smiles. "You will make my family very happy. Thank you."

She hugs me then and I feel how much love she has in her heart. With her arms around me, I understand that we do have a connection and I feel so happy and energized to be in the presence of someone so full of joy. I wake up at 3:12 A.M., feeling puzzled and confused about what just happened to me. Who was she? She said I reminded her of her grandfather. Later in the day, once I'm fully awake, I wrote these notes to recall my experience.

In a follow-up correspondence, Albert explained that this dream visitation happened just two days after the loss of his brother's granddaughter, Adelia Rose Williams. He'd never had the opportunity to meet her because of a family feud with his brother's wife. "My brother's wife chose to distance her children from the rest of the family," he said, "and I had no way to get a hold of them, no correspondence for so many years."

And still, as Adelia's spirit indicated in the dream, he was soon visited by his brother's family. Out of the blue, Albert's niece, Natalia, who is Adelia's living mother, was visiting Houston, where

Albert lives. He recalled, "It was a big shocker when my niece, Natalia, visited me in Houston, and I quickly wanted to let her know of my special dream experience. I finally understood that the message was meant for her. I sat and read her my notes and Natalia filled in the pieces of the story I did not know. She explained that her daughter, Adelia, died of the very rare disease known as Hutchinson-Gilford progeria syndrome, a condition that causes rapid aging. She was, in fact, fifteen years old when she passed. I was told she had lost the use of one eye and struggled to move her body. She'd also lost much of her hair as the disease often causes alopecia, total hair loss. One of her most wishful desires was to have real hair, like her mom's. Before Natalia left, I gave her a copy of my dream notes. Later, Natalia sent me this email."

> I took the time to read your notes, and I was once again touched and emotional. The dream you had of Adelia sounds so much like her. Your conversation with her in this dream made me feel as if she was actually talking to you, as you describe how she would express her usual joy and happy mannerisms, and her strong desire to be healthy and to have her natural hair. For the rest of my life, I will be thankful that you shared this special moment with me. The experience not only brought tears to my eyes, but it also brought me some peace and warmth. Thank God my baby is finally happy, and her inner beauty came out at last.

Adelia's lesson for all of us is that real beauty is within, and it is our collective work to recognize it in ourselves and in others. Spirit reminds me that our outsides are an illusion. We have a body;

we are a soul. Now that she's free of her physical body, Adelia can truly celebrate her beauty, her love and light within, and my intuitive sense is that her dream visitation will begin to heal old wounds throughout Albert's family line.

Grow the Feeling through Inspired Action

• • •

When we shine our inner light, our energetic vibration naturally rises and attracts those people in our soul group into our present-day orbit who are a vibrational match. While it is true that we tend to learn our most meaningful lessons through hardship, the end goal is not to stay in conflict but to graduate to the next level in our lives, where we're surrounded by a majority of people in our soul group who inspire feelings of safety, confidence, worthiness, harmony, happiness, and deep connection, and where we feel seen and heard, empowered, valued, and loved. This is when we are in the company of our Earth angels, and with them by our side, we can more easily finish this round of Earth School with grace and ease.

Sounds heavenly, doesn't it?

It gets even better. To take this inspired action, all you have to do is lead by example.

Day to day, be mindful of your energy and take responsibility for what you broadcast out into the world, and what you're attracting to you. Day to day, make the conscious choice to respond rather than react to people and situations. Practice neutrality. Consider what the echoes and patterns in your life are showing you, in order to teach you. Embrace the work. Make mistakes and keep going. Trust that you are connected and surrounded. When in doubt, ask for guidance: show me the next right step forward. When in fear, ask yourself: *What would love do?*

When you have your answer, do that.

When we commit day after day to be in energetic alignment with the high frequency of love and light within us, it becomes an effortless action to elevate the people and the world around us. And this is how we make Heaven a place on Earth.

CHAPTER 9

Share Your Notes

...

For a recent birthday gift, Chris surprised me with tickets to the Coachella festival. While being in large crowds isn't exactly my idea of heaven, we both love music and travel, and value our alone time together, so I accepted the present and began to plan for our adventure.

But as our weekend approached, I found myself experiencing a familiar sense of dread. As an empath and an intuitive, the frenetic energy of crowds overwhelms me. Against my better judgment and disregarding a boundary I'd set long ago about going to these types of events, I'd volunteered to do something I didn't actually want to do. And furthermore, I wondered, *Why did Chris commit us to three full, ten-hour days of concert-size crowds in one-hundred-degree heat?* He knows me better than this, and that I'd rather spend a quiet day alone with him in a place where we could just relax. I started to feel the type of resentment I've historically paired with not feeling seen and heard, but instead of telling Chris I wanted to cancel our weekend plans, I decided to ask for higher guidance.

The night before our trip, I excused myself from the living room, where our family was watching TV, and retreated upstairs to our bedroom. I sat in quiet meditation for almost an hour and asked my guides to help me create my version of Heaven on Earth within the parameters of the tightly packed, weekend lineup. Instead of focusing on the details, I clarified how I wanted to *feel*—joyful, relaxed, safe, and connected to myself, to Chris, and to Spirit. I let go of how this would look, specifically, and put my faith and trust in the bigger plan unfolding behind the scenes. And for good measure, I asked my guides to "please protect my energy should I get stuck in an endless line for the portable bathrooms."

The next afternoon, we landed in Palm Springs and headed straight to the rental car counter. The first good sign was that the only car available to us was a red Mustang convertible—*the iconic symbol of freedom and fun!*—and we happily hopped in and hit the road. The festival is held about twenty-five miles southeast of Palm Springs in Riverside County. Not a long distance to travel except that about halfway there, traffic came to a standstill, and our app estimated it would take us three hours to drive the last ten miles. *Three hours?!* I took a deep breath, and just as I was about to resign myself to spending the afternoon sitting bumper-to-bumper with thousands of other festivalgoers, Chris said, "Screw it. Let's turn around and go to dinner instead."

Now that was more like it.

We headed back into Palm Springs and found a lovely Greek restaurant where we could hear live music playing on the garden patio. I asked Chris if he was sorry to miss out on the first concert day. "We may have already missed Billie Eilish and Harry Styles," I said. Two artists that we'd specifically hoped to see.

Chris shrugged. "I'm cool with it." And he nodded at the guy playing acoustic guitar on the patio. "I kind of hate to admit it, but this is more my speed." We laughed at ourselves, and by the end of our very chill evening, we recommitted to Day Two of the festival. "Tomorrow, we're all in," we agreed. But the next morning Chris surprised me again. Instead of gearing up to head out for the day, Chris suggested we lie by the pool and soak up the sun, an activity I always enjoy. I smiled to myself, wondering if my guides were inspiring him. Either way, I happily agreed to hang by the pool, and when we finally made it to the festival later that afternoon, I felt 100 percent ready to be there. My energy was up, and I was open to "whatever happens."

Our intention was to embrace the scene and find a spot for ourselves in it. And yet, so many people. So many selfies. So much posturing. About an hour into it, Chris turned to me and said, "I don't know about you, but I've had my fill. . . . Wanna go?"

I smiled. "Yes, please, let's get out of here."

On the third and final day of our getaway, we both agreed to skip the festival entirely and hike at Joshua Tree National Forest. I'd woken up unintentionally at 6:28, which is my birth date and my numeric "sign" from Spirit. I'd also logged three hours and thirty-three minutes of REM sleep according to a sleeping app on my phone. This caught my attention because in my world of the weird, a sequence of threes (333) means "mastery," where one is grounded in their power, learning their lessons, and supported by ascended masters on the Other Side. The numbers were clearly lining up for a day of miracles and flow. But to be sure, I asked my Team Spirit to clearly make their presence known. A sizeable order, but why not ask for what you want? And what do you know, the first indicator that we were being guided from beyond was when Chris turned the ignition on our rental car and the mileage was parked at 33,333. Adding to that, we soon pulled behind a car with the license plate: 628. A sequence of threes and my birthday numbers, again. I tell you—ask and you shall receive.

I'd wanted to go to Joshua Tree since the legendary U2 album of the same name came out in the 1980s. On the drive out to the forest, we played *The Joshua Tree* in its entirety while singing along. During "I Still Haven't Found What I'm Looking For," I hit pause and skipped back to a lyric I hadn't remembered where Bono describes the "Kingdom come" as a place where "all the colors bleed into one." I thought about how Spirit uses the rainbow as a sign for "heaven," where all the colors of the rainbow come together as one high vibrational frequency where we're connected by love, as love. As the song played on, I couldn't help but feel that we were entering a magical place. And, as if to validate this feeling, the first person we saw in the park was a man wearing a T-shirt with one word: HEAVENLY.

Chris and I spent eight hours hiking and driving through the expansive park, and the signs that appeared along our path were nothing less than magical. At one point, we pulled over at Queen Ranch, which seemed appropriate, as one of my newest spirit guides identifies herself as "queen." We sat outside the car and meditated on the natural beauty, the stillness and limitlessness of the desert. I truly felt connected to something bigger than myself and was reminded that we don't need to go anywhere, really, to connect to Spirit. We only need to stop and be still. To be here now. Chris and I agreed that we felt as if we'd stepped out of time, that Joshua Tree was some kind of vortex that warped

3D reality, but the truth is that we hadn't slipped into another dimension or walked through a portal. Rather, we were wide-awake in present space and time. Presence can be easy to miss because we're so conditioned to future-trip and slip back into the past. Being truly in the moment can feel unfamiliar.

And blissfully intense.

With the sun on my face, I stretched my arms out wide, taking in the abundance and sense of freedom that is Joshua Tree. I consciously set the intention to shift my beliefs about scarcity and lack into gratitude for this slice of Heaven on Earth. I mentally affirmed: *I am holding my worth. I trust that I am Divinely held and cared for, and capable of giving and receiving freely in the abundance of all things.* I climbed to the top of a nearby rock formation and symbolically stood my ground and reminded myself that in order to protect our energy, we must each set boundaries to maintain seniority over our light. Whereas the night before Chris and I were waffling about the festival, falling into the trap of judgment and feeling the pressure of what we "should" do—I now understood that we were exactly where we were supposed to be. I thanked my guides for providing us with the opportunity to connect and align with the I AM presence within, and to feel safe to just *be*.

For the next several hours, Chris and I continued to drive through the park, pulling over to hike, hopping back in our car, and fully enjoying the ride. Finally, as we exited the park, we noticed a house with the following address: 62828. My birthday numbers, again, and impossible to miss because the address plaque was huge! I grabbed my phone to take a picture and the time was 3:33 P.M.! I burst into tears and thanked my guides for so many clear signs throughout the day. As we traveled back through the desert toward our hotel, I thought about our experience, a slice of heaven, and I was reminded that heaven is whatever brings you a sense of deep comfort, peace, relief, contentment, and joy. As Chris drove us back into "civilization," I scribbled the following into my journal:

> Trust that you are *there* when you feel this space and place within your heart. One of our greatest gifts in this lifetime is our free will, the freedom to choose, and that includes the choice to *remember* our inherent worthiness and engage with others and the world at the highest frequency of love. Elisabeth Kübler Ross wrote that "all positive emotions come from love," and we choose heaven every time we say no to fear and choose love instead.

Well, the next morning, I was called to walk my talk. I'd been on a spiritual high, and now, I could feel myself slipping into the low frequency of fear as we headed to the airport. Reentry after a vacation can quickly get me down. I start to miss the experience I just had and future-trip about what's coming next. I used to feel this way a lot as a kid. Every summer I would visit my grandparents in Los Angeles, and when it was time to travel back home to Omaha, I would cry the farther away we got from the ocean, one of my happiest places. Where my lifelong habit has been to numb my pain, I resisted the urge to ask Chris to drive through Starbucks for a supercharged sugar-and-caffeine-filled drink. Instead, I leaned into my fear. It felt like a hole burning my stomach wall even without the acidity from coffee. When

Chris glanced over and registered the discomfort on my face, he asked me what was wrong. I tearfully confessed that I was sad to go home, to leave this magical place and space for us. He put his hand on mine and squeezed it. "It's been awesome and now, on to the next." He wasn't dismissing my feelings, only reaffirming what I already knew. Our lives will continue to move forward, presenting us with new opportunities every day. Good or bad, wanted or unwanted, where you are, what you have, who you're with, what you're doing, how you're feeling, is not forever. And yet, we can take comfort in what comes *next*.

As we continued our drive toward the airport, I smiled as I recalled one of my favorite quotes by Dr. Seuss: "Don't cry because it's over; smile because it happened." I mentally thanked my guides for helping me to see the experience through the lens of love, for the gift of this trip, and for the time to recharge and reconnect to my most important relationships—to Spirit, to myself, and to my partner. By the time we boarded the plane, I felt whole and ready to return to our house full of six kids and to my work, which reminds me every day that I AM here to teach, to learn, to heal, and to serve. And that I, like anyone else, am human and that when I make mistakes (which is how Earth School is designed), I AM worthy of forgiveness, kindness, and compassion. I AM worthy of another chance, the opportunity to begin again. Like everyone else, I'm still plugging along, doing the work and I AM worthy of loving myself along the way.

In several meditations since the Joshua Tree trip, I've been nudged to wear white, which is weird, because black is my go-to. My guides have shown me that wearing white will remind me to be the light in the dark, and to recognize the light in others. Even I can sometimes forget that we're all energetic light beings connected to the biggest energy source that exists, one that vibrates with all the best feels—acceptance, unity, joy, peace, and love—and when spirits get to the Other Side, they remember this truth. That they are home.

You can remember it now.

You don't have to die or go anywhere special to experience a heavenly existence. Heaven is here, now. It is vibrating within you. And it will blow the doors off your life as soon as you tune in and *feel* it.

Graduation Day
Rainbow Meditation

• • •

Meditation is a practice. And the more you practice, the more attuned and harmonized you become to a higher vibration. And the more harmonized you are, the easier and faster it is for you to cocreate your heavenly life. Even if you feel like nothing is happening or that you're not receiving any messages or impressions, trust in the knowledge that you're changing your frequency so that *after meditation*, in your daily life, you're in alignment with 5D energy. And when you're in sync with this higher, faster vibrational energy, life begins to yield to you ongoing synchronicities, signs, miracles, and flow.

In this meditation we're going to go deep and wide to ground, connect, clear, expand, and protect our entire being.

We'll start by **grounding** our energy, and then **connecting** to Spirit, to come into alignment with our higher self and Spirit energy.

Then, we'll **clear** the distractions or energetic debris that are holding us back from experiencing our desired intentions.

Next, we'll **expand** our energy by puffing up our aura and running rainbow light throughout our body and all four layers of our energy field. Doing so helps to call in our intentions, so that our experiences begin to reflect our intentions, in cocreation with the Divine.

From there, we'll **protect** our entire being-body and aura by bubble-wrapping ourselves in golden white light, and placing golden mirrors around us, like being inside a giant disco ball. This helps to deflect any negative lower vibrational energies around us while sending out our light to the world around us.

And finally, we'll complete the process by placing our order with Spirit and the Universe, setting clear intentions on what we want to call in to **cocreate** our idea of a "Heavenly Life."

 # Meditation

• • •

Start by closing your eyes and getting into a comfortable position. Sit up with your spine straight, your hands resting on your lap, and feet flat on the ground, or lie down.

Take a few deep centering breaths as you draw your attention inward, getting present in this moment now. Set the intention to relax every muscle in your body from the top of your head to the tips of your toes. As you inhale and exhale, notice your breathing; notice the rhythm of it for a moment. Be aware of any sounds around you; whatever you hear from now on will only serve to relax you. And as you exhale, release any tension and stress you may be holding on to. As you inhale, imagine a cleansing white light washing away any stressful thoughts in your mind; begin to feel them melt away, allowing for a deep sense of inner peace and relaxation. Notice how very comfortable your body feels, just drifting and floating, deeper, deeper, deeper relaxed.

Now, I want you to imagine yourself getting "spiritually dressed" for your graduation day, which marks all of the hard work and growth you've done on every level of your being, allowing you to ascend up and into your Divine Spirit, and fully embody YOU!

(Grounding)

Imagine that you are putting on a graduation gown or robe made of every color of the rainbow. See your whole body covered and then filled and illuminated with this rainbow light. Every cell and aspect of your being vibrates at the frequency of this rainbow light. This robe has rainbow ribbons extending from it, going down past your feet, into the earth, like the roots of a tree, bringing with it rainbow ribbons of light that anchor you deep into the core of Earth. These rainbow ribbons vibrate at a very powerful, full-spectrum light frequency, allowing you to feel grounded and divinely held by Mother Earth (or Mama Gaia).

Mentally declare: I AM now grounded in my body, fully present and in my power.

(Connecting)

Next, place a graduation cap, appearing as a crown of light, on top of your head, made of pure gold. This gold crown vibrates at the frequency of creativity, truth, and love. Visualize a rainbow tassel that extends upward like a ribbon or cord of rainbow light, tethering you to a golden sun above, the energy of Spirit. This rainbow light travels back down the tassel, into your crown, causing your mind to open and expand as this light swirls rainbow energy mixed with golden sparkles of light, activating your Divine knowing (or Divinity) and connection to Spirit.

Mentally declare: I AM now connected to the love and light of Spirit.

(Clearing)

Now pull through **royal blue,** from the top of your head down to your feet, to rinse away any and all fears and limitation . . . letting it calm your nervous system, pulling you into a place of peace, clarity, and calm. At the same time, you are pushing away any and all energetic debris from your being and your space . . . releasing illusion, delusion, confusion, insecurity, and fear. Mentally call all your energy back to you—from any person, spirit, or place—calling it back from the past and the future. Demand that all your energy come back to you—your creativity, prosperity, abundance, sovereignty, joy, peace, faith, and trust—call it all back now.

Be here now and feel this blue light wash you clean, and as it does, it allows your chakras, made up of all the colors of the rainbow, to shine more brightly.

Mentally declare: I AM now energetically cleansed and cleared, attuned to my Divine wellness code.

(Expanding)

And now this rainbow light flows down this tassel/cord on your crown into each of your seven main chakras, located along your spinal column, incorporating rainbow light into each energy center. Just observe how this high-frequency rainbow light calibrates and upgrades each chakra to the level that's in alignment with your highest good right now. Now see this rainbow light radiating out to and filling all four layers of your being—*Physical, Mental, Emotional, and Spiritual being.* You begin to glow and radiate this energy of Divinity in its highest expression.

Mentally declare: I AM now ascending up and into my soul's highest evolution.

(Protecting)

Now with your intention and attention, imagine bubble-wrapping yourself—body and aura, which extends in all directions and as far as your outstretched arms—in a sparkly gold light. With each breath, your bubble expands in size and power, getting bigger, brighter, and lighter in all directions. This protective bubble serves as an energetic shield that doesn't allow anything of a lower vibe to penetrate it.

Now imagine a giant golden mirrored disco ball encompassing this protective bubble, allowing you to safely shine your rainbow light from the inside out while deflecting and purifying anything less than light and love from your space.

Mentally declare: I AM now protected as I AM Divinely held in the light and love of Spirit.

(Creating)

Now, say your full name three times *(either out loud or to yourself)*, bringing your conscious awareness and creative capability into this present moment to create your intentions. . . .

Now, with your intention and attention, ask yourself, *What do I want to create in my life? What do I want to call in? What is my idea of a heavenly life?* Take a moment and set your intention ... envision in your mind's eye (sixth chakra) what your life looks like, in a perfect world, if you were to experience this intention.

Create a story now—a mental movie—of what that looks like and feels like, as if it were your reality right now, as if all things are possible.

Just hold these thoughts and feelings for seventeen seconds—the approximate time it takes to effectively send out vibrational energy to the Universe. The Universe responds to our dominant thoughts and feelings.

Really get into your heart, and FEEL this intention, with a deep sense of gratitude and relief, that you are fully embodying and living your intention, right here, right now.

Now with your intention and attention, imagine placing your intentions of a Heavenly Life into Spirit's hands.

And now say: I ask for this or something more, with ease and grace, for the highest and best good for all.

And now turn your attention to the golden sun above your head, and turn it up to bright orange, purifying and amplifying your energy, returning you to *your* original Divine wellness code, and correcting it back to *your* Divine Truth.

We ask that as you move out of this meditation, that your every thought, word, and deed be a reflection of your intention, bringing it into creation with ease and grace, and in gratitude.

So be it, it is done, and we give thanks for a heavenly life on Earth.

Acknowledgments

• • •

As with all my creative undertakings, I prefer it to be an organic process where Spirit takes the lead, inspiring me with the Divine guidance and wisdom that will best serve those ready to receive. And the cocreation of this book was no exception. The idea for this book was inspired by both my husband, Christian, acting as a messenger on behalf of my guides in Spirit, and through the many readings I've done over the past couple of years involving this concept of soul contracts. I remain profoundly grateful and humbled to be a messenger for Spirit, and would not have been able to impart this spiritual wisdom if it weren't for my "Team Spirit," both in Heaven and on Earth.

Samantha Rose, my talented writing partner and beloved friend, whose invaluable writing expertise and creative genius helped to shape the wisdom and magic held in these pages. I'm forever grateful for her willingness to rise to the occasion once again, and stretch and grow with me as we embarked on this labor of love.

Yfat Reiss Gendell, my literary agent, dear friend, and greatest cheerleader, who continues to push me past my comfort zone with her encouragement and vision of what's possible. I'm thankful we've been able to evolve together, through this project in particular, allowing us both the opportunity to rise up and into more of our power and light. And a big thanks to the team at YRG

Partners—Ashley Napier, Sara DeNobrega, and the many foreign coagents who have supported my work for over a decade. I'm grateful to you for the ongoing help in getting my books into the hands of the many translation readers around the world who have responded to the work described in these pages.

This book would not be what it is if not for the vision, wisdom, and expertise of my rock star editor, Julie Will. Her thoughtful guidance and genius editorial input have made this a stronger book, and she has continually gone the extra mile to ensure the intended thoughts and ideas are clearly reflected in a compelling and authentic narrative. Julie has made this process both enjoyable and smooth as we worked together to bring this creation to light.

Karen Rinaldi, my publisher, and the wonderful team at Harper Wave, including Yelena Nesbit, Amanda Pritzker, Leah Carlson-Stanisic, Robin Bilardello, Nikki Baldauf, and Emma Kupor. I thank them all for their enthusiasm, support, and faith in me and the evolution of this book. I consider myself extremely blessed to have had this opportunity to share my message with the world at a time of great Universal need, and recognize their role in making this dream a reality.

My amazing RRE team, Elizabeth Buckius, Hannah Brown, and Kwame Johnson—each of them continues to bring a unique skill set and creative genius to the table, allowing me to continue reaching and growing my audience with a level of quality and care that's reflected in all we do. My professional success is largely the result in part of their ongoing support, organization, invaluable input, and care.

My colleague and treasured friend, Gabrielle Bernstein, who has graciously taken me under her wing by imparting both her spiritual and business wisdom over the past decade, allowing me to soar higher and shine brighter. I am beyond grateful for her being a part of my Ground Crew, always having my back, and, more important, reminding me that the Universe has my back!

I owe much of my sanity and spiritual evolution these past four years to my energy healer, mentor, and soul sister, Jakki Smith Leonardini. I am blessed to share her invaluable insights and spiritual knowledge imparted in this book, serving to empower and inspire any reader. Her love, support, and faith in me have lifted me higher, allowing me to embody more of my soul light, and in turn be of greater service to the world, and for that I am deeply grateful.

My beloved husband, Christian, who has served as one of my greatest polishing stones, pillars of strength, and love of my life, who inspires me every day to keep doing the work to learn, grow, and evolve into a better human. He has taught me how to love deeper, laugh more, and live fully, embracing each moment with a grateful heart, while keeping our love on top, as we continue to create our heavenly life together.

My children, Jakob, Sam, and Haven, along with my bonus stepchildren, Hannah, Hadley, and Harper, who continue to help me keep my feet on the ground, despite being in the business of working in the clouds! Each one of them is uniquely themselves—perfectly imperfect—and I am grateful for their willingness to openly share their personal stories with readers, recognizing the opportunity to help inspire others as a result. They continue to be my greatest teachers, and for that I feel blessed.

I wouldn't be the person I am today without the unconditional love and support of my mother, Jan, and stepdad, Howard, who remain my greatest cheerleaders. My mom continues to inspire me by her shining example in choosing to show up each day with a positive attitude, open heart, and passionately contributing to making the world a better place.

To all the rest of my "ground crew"—

My brother, Zach Perelman, and brother and sister-in-law Baruch and Ariela HaLevi—whose support, wisdom, and guidance continue to center, ground, and inspire me forward; my team of healers: Celeste Williamson, Dr. Janet Settle, Clark Reddick, Wendy Kelley, Ariel Hardy, and Dr. Jen Vitaro; Laura Love & GroundFloor media team, all my amigas, soul sisters, and dear friends—their ongoing love, support, expertise, and presence in my life continue to lift me higher, allowing me to live a more balanced, grounded, and wholehearted life, evolving into more of who I am as we walk this path together.

My Team Spirit—MC, M3, M5; and my father, Shelly, and all other ancestors and angels working behind the scenes to bless and assist me in fulfilling my soul contract, with grace, ease, and joy . . . please know I am eternally grateful and always willing to receive!

My deepest thanks go out to all my clients, family, and friends who bravely shared their stories in this book, along with all my clients who have come to me over the years with an open mind and heart, allowing me the opportunity to share my healing work. It is my hope that through their experiences and growth shared within these pages, others will be comforted, healed, and inspired. And to all my colleagues who continue to support and inspire me, thank you. Each of you is as much a part of my soul contract as I am yours, and for that I am truly humbled and grateful.

To all of the above, deep and heartfelt thanks, brightest blessings, and all love.

Namaste
Rebecca Rosen

Conversation Questions
for Life Review

...

Dear reader, the following Life Review questions were ex-
changed between my husband, Chris, and his dad to facili-
tate healing in their relationship, and as I shared in the opening
chapter, they really did help to break the ice and begin a warming
between them. If you're so inclined, they can similarly be used
in your life to prompt conversations that allow for an honest
inventory of your relationships with Spirit, self, and others and
that inspire clarity, healing connection, and closure. Before starting, I would suggest setting the stage with an intention of creating a sacred, safe space, allowing only Divine energy into your
experience, while getting out of your head and dropping into
your heart where you connect with pure, healing energy. Consider saying a brief prayer, inviting Spirit in, and aligning with
your higher self to ensure the conversation is coming from the

frequency of love, truth, and compassion, with the intention for the highest good for all.

1. Heaven is a feeling, and it's different for everyone. What does *your* heaven feel like? What does it look like?

2. Who is there to greet you? Who are the people, animals, and/or your Team Spirit waiting to give you a warm welcome home?

3. What in your life are you most proud of?

4. What in your life do you most regret?

5. Who has been your greatest hero/mentor/teacher, and why?

6. What lessons have you learned in this lifetime?

7. Which of those lessons is a work in progress and which are not yet complete?

8. Which of those lessons are you most proud of completing?

9. What's the greatest obstacle or challenge you overcame, and what was the gift in it?

10. What do you regret having done?

11. What do you regret that you did not do?

12. If you could replay this lifetime and change only a few things, what would you change?

13. Who would you like to apologize to that you have not?

14. Who do you wish would apologize *to you* who hasn't?

15. *I'm sorry, I love you, please forgive me.* Who in your life would you like to say this to before you die?

16. How do you feel about our relationship?

17. What regrets do you have in our relationship, such as things left unsaid and/or undone?

18. What would you say to me, if they were to be your final words?

19. Are you open to hear what I have to say to you?

20. What are the positive and negative legacies that you inherited?

21. What are the positive and negative legacies that you are leaving behind?

22. What are a few of your perceived biggest failures, disappointments, or regrets?

23. What do you feel you have done to help heal your ancestral lineage of any negative patterns, behaviors, or mindsets?

24. What are you doing differently and better than the example you had at the time?

25. What ancestral patterns do you feel you have consciously or unconsciously perpetuated?

26. What is one thing you can pass on to your family that will help to free them from any dysfunctional karmic cycle?

27. If you could tell your fifteen-year-old self one thing, what would it be?

28. If you had to sum up your life in one word or phrase, what would it be?

29. How has your life made a difference in this world?

30. If you had to leave behind three invaluable lessons or insights that you learned during your lifetime that you would want people to know or remember you by, what would they be?

About the Author

. . .

Internationally acclaimed bestselling author, spiritual medium, and speaker **REBECCA ROSEN** has made it her mission to open the line of communication between the spirit world and our day-to-day world. Her incredibly accurate and detailed readings have amazed and empowered clients and led Rebecca to national media appearances on *The Dr. Oz Show*, *E! News* specials, *Fox & Friends*, *Dr. Phil*, *Entertainment Tonight*, *Extra*, *Nightline*, and *The Rachael Ray Show*, among other outlets. She was also on the Lifetime Movie Network show *The Last Goodbye*. Rebecca has written three books: *Spirited*, *Awaken the Spirit Within*, and *What the Dead Have Taught Me About Living Well*. She recently started a podcast, *Small Medium at Large*, that explores many facets of our connection with our "team spirit" on the other side. Rebecca resides in Denver with her husband and children.

Bonus Material

• • •

Scan this QR code to access free bonus material in the form of guided meditations, instructional videos, and custom assessments based on the exercises in the book.